Alicia Tycer

Caryl Churchill's
Top Girls

continuum

Continuum

The Tower Building, 11 York Road, London SE1 7NX

80 Maiden Lane, Suite 704, New York NY 10038

www.continuumbooks.com

First published 2008

British Library Cataloguing-in-Publication Data
A catalogue record for this book is available from the British Library.

ISBN: 978-0-8264-9555-6 (hardback)
       978-0-8264-9556-3 (paperback)

Library of Congress Cataloging-in-Publication Data
A catalog record for this book is available from the Library of Congress

Typeset by Kenneth Burnley, Wirral, Cheshire
Printed and bound in Great Britain by MPG Books Ltd, Bodmin, Cornwall

Contents

General Preface vii

Acknowledgements ix

1 Background and Context 1

2 Analysis and Commentary 23

3 Production History 71

4 Workshopping the Play 85

5 Conclusion 101

Timeline 105

Notes 113

Further Reading 119

References 123

Index 129

General Preface

Continuum Modern Theatre Guides

Volumes in the series Continuum Modern Theatre Guides offer concise and informed introductions to the key plays of modern times. Each book takes a close look at one particular play's dramaturgical qualities and then at its various theatrical manifestations. The books are carefully structured to offer a systematic study of the play in its biographical, historical, social and political context, followed by an in-depth study of the text and a chapter which outlines the work's production history, examining both the original productions of the play and subsequent major stage interpretations. Where relevant, screen adaptations will also be analysed. There then follows a chapter dedicated to workshopping the play, based on suggested group exercises. Also included are a timeline and suggestions for further reading.

Each book covers:

- Background and context
- Analysis of the play
- Production history
- Workshopping exercises

The aim is to provide accessible introductions to modern plays for students in both Theatre/Performance Studies and English, as well as for informed general readers. The series includes up-to-date coverage of a broad range of key plays, with summaries of important critical approaches and the intellectual debates that have illuminated the meaning of the work and made a significant contribution to our broader cultural life. They will enable readers to develop their understanding of playwrights and theatre-makers, as well as inspiring them to broaden their studies.

The Editors:
Steve Barfield, Janelle Reinelt,
Graham Saunders and Aleks Sierz

March 2008

Acknowledgements

Methuen Drama (A&C Black Publishers Ltd) allowed me to cite from the text of *Top Girls* used in *Caryl Churchill Plays: 2*. I would like to acknowledge Michael Daniels for permission to print his photo of Bianca Amato as Marlene from the Guthrie 1996 production of *Top Girls* on the cover of this book. Of course I would also like to acknowledge Caryl Churchill for writing such a thought-provoking play.

I would very much like to thank Janelle Reinelt for inspiring my interest in Caryl Churchill and for her numerous helpful suggestions during the writing process of this book. I am grateful to Elaine Aston and Graham Saunders for their welcoming generosity and knowledge while researching in the UK. I would also like to thank faculty members at the University of California, Irvine and University of California, San Diego for their encouragement, especially Bryan Reynolds, John Rouse, Nadine George, Laura O'Connor and Jim Carmody.

Personally, I would like to express my gratitude to Kandace Korth and Gordon Wiser for providing me with wonderful getaways where I could write in peace. Thank you to Patricia Wilshire and Caroline Brooks for always welcoming me to London. Many thanks to Genny Blewett, Golnag Tahsini and Mark Alkons for their assistance during the writing process. Thanks to Janna Segal for many late-night conversations. Finally, but definitely not least, many thanks to my family for their ongoing support, especially my brother Vince for sharing my interest in all things dramatic, my father Bert for always talking to me about politics, and most of all, my mother for exposing me to the joys of the theatre.

To my parents, Jayne and Bert Tycer

1 Background and Context

This chapter provides the reader with the background information that will be useful in understanding *Top Girls*. First, the chapter outlines the primary reasons for the play's ongoing significance. Next, it examines Caryl Churchill's prolific playwriting career, providing pertinent biographical details and discussing a selection of her plays, highlighting their thematic and stylistic relevance to *Top Girls*. Finally, the chapter looks at the social, political and historical context of Britain during the early 1980s, when the play was first performed. Particular attention is paid to exploring the socialist and feminist movements and to tracking the political career of Margaret Thatcher.

Why *Top Girls* is important

Caryl Churchill once wrote: 'Playwrights don't give answers, they ask questions.'[1] In *Top Girls*, one of her most significant works, Churchill asks: Is it more important to break out of a cycle of poverty and 'make something of yourself', or to fulfil your responsibilities to your family and community? If you are a woman, are you more likely to answer this question in a certain way? How can women balance the demands of a career and motherhood? What actually constitutes success in life? First staged in 1982, *Top Girls* has become emblematic of contemporary woman's ongoing struggles with such issues.

Churchill wrote the play as a response to the election of Margaret Thatcher. Although some viewed Thatcher's rise to political power as indicative of progress for women, Churchill worried that Thatcher's right-wing politics benefited a minority of wealthy Britons while leaving the less fortunate behind. The play voices Churchill's concerns regarding a societal emphasis on capitalist success over sisterly solidarity. In order to confront the era's broad ranging political dilemmas, she compares and contrasts the lives of two sisters. Each of these women has different answers to the questions the play asks: while one sister decides to follow a path that emphasizes her career at the expense of her family life, the other maintains close familial ties but continues to lead a life of economic drudgery. Churchill avoids idealizing either path, but her portrayal presents an opportunity for her audiences to examine their opinions regarding gender and class. Furthermore, her depiction of a troubled future generation provides a poignant reminder of the importance of social responsibility.

Top Girls is renowned not only for its political commentary, but also for its stylistic innovations. As a writer, Churchill tends to use multiple experiments in style and form. In *Top Girls*, she establishes the principle of overlapping dialogue, a technique that has become widespread in contemporary British theatre. Furthermore, the play presents scenes out of sequential order, thereby requiring the audience to actively participate by connecting the play's plot lines. The first act depicts a transhistorical tableau in which Marlene, an eighties' career woman, hosts a dinner party for a table full of disparate women drawn from history, literature and art. The next two acts focus on Marlene's career and family life during the 1980s, with the last act being set a year before the previous act. In the first production, actors were cast as both contemporary and historical characters, a precedent which subsequent productions have followed. The play's radically non-linear narrative structure and multiple-role casting leads to the potential for multiple interpretations, encouraging viewers to compare and contrast recent and historical moments.

With *Top Girls*, Churchill achieved the tenuous balance of addressing feminist politics and appealing to popular audiences. Within the male-dominated theatre environment, Churchill placed women's concerns unapologetically centre stage. Additionally, the play's all-female cast provides opportunities for actresses to portray complex characters. While all-female productions were in vogue among feminist groups during the 1980s, few gained *Top Girls'* level of popular success or critical acclaim. Indeed, theatre scholar Dimple Godiwala argues that the all-female production meant that 'the *writing* of *Top Girls* was the single most conscious intervention that British feminist dramaturgy was to make on the patriarchal mode of dramatic discourse' (2003, p. 8). Thus, the play was at once highly original and unusual, and is still without significant equal in the feminist or mainstream canons.

The 1982 staging at the Royal Court Theatre, directed by Max Stafford-Clark, was a landmark production. The play's successful transferral to New York confirmed Churchill's relevance on both sides of the Atlantic, and its widespread success helped forge a path for future women playwrights. As the newspaper critic Benedict Nightingale puts it: 'After *Top Girls* it was no longer possible to patronize "women dramatists" as some promising but lesser species of creative creature.'[2] Although his comment says as much about the critics' preconceptions of women playwrights as it does about the merit of the play itself, it does indicate the crucial shift in perception that *Top Girls* facilitated. The play was nominated for the Susan Smith Blackburn Prize and was the recipient of multiple Obie Awards, and continues to resonate with audiences, being frequently revived in professional and amateur productions worldwide.

Now considered a contemporary classic, *Top Girls* is included in school curricula and drama anthologies as both representing feminist theatre during the 1980s and exhibiting ongoing relevance. Mainstream publications such as Christopher Innes'

Modern British Drama (2002) as well as works examining the specifically feminist canon such as Helene Keyssar's *Feminist Theatre* (1984) analyse the play's significance. The questions the play raises contributed significantly to the ongoing process of defining feminist theatre, encouraging feminists to re-examine and engage in the process of defining their priorities. Feminist theatre scholar Lizbeth Goodman lists the play as an exemplary member of the feminist canon because of its experiments in form and the way in which it reclaims women's voices from history. She argues that *Top Girls* was so effective because the play reached people outside of the feminist movement and focused public attention on concerns of real-life working women who were not being provided with adequate resources (1993, p. 227).

Top Girls is arguably even more pertinent today than when it was first produced. Indeed, scholars often consider the work prophetic, predicting much of the British class struggle of the 1980s and also the increasing disparity in wealth, which continues into the new century. In a post-feminist landscape, the play's criticisms of hard-nosed individualism suggest possibilities for a renewed sense of political mobilization. The play continues to resonate with audiences, and emerging playwrights frequently cite the play as an inspiration. For example, Mark Ravenhill, who wrote the Royal Court's hit *Shopping and Fucking*, declares: 'I read *Top Girls* at least once a year and I weep. One day, I think, one day I'll write something as good.'[3]

Caryl Churchill's biography

Caryl Churchill is widely considered to be one of the most innovative playwrights to have emerged in post-war British theatre. In the span of her prolific career, she has garnered both popular successes and critical respect. Indeed, Churchill is one of a select number of playwrights whose work receives acclaim from both British and international audiences. Having often worked with feminist, socialist and experimental theatre groups, she is also one of the few British women playwrights to have her plays incorporated into the dramatic canon. Churchill started writing when very few women were having plays produced professionally, and continues to write provocative works that challenge dramatic conventions.

Churchill was born in London on 3 September 1938. When she was nine, she moved with her family to Canada, where she attended the Trafalgar School, Montreal. As an only child, she enjoyed writing short stories and poems, inventing characters and attending the theatre.[4] Churchill had a middle-class upbringing, and cites her father Robert Churchill's work as a political cartoonist as an influence.[5] Unlike the career woman portrayed in *Top Girls*, her parents raised Churchill to aspire towards both a career and motherhood. After leaving school at 14, Churchill's mother had worked as a secretary, model and actress, and continued performing bit parts after her daughter was born. Churchill recalled that her mother 'did talk to me about working, and the fact that she used not to wear her wedding ring to work. I had the feeling, rather early on, that having a career was in no way incompatible with staying married and being very happy.'[6]

After spending her adolescence in Canada, Churchill returned to England in 1956 to attend Lady Margaret Hall, Oxford, from where she received a Bachelor of Arts degree in English Language and Literature and was awarded the Richard Hillary Memorial Prize. While at Oxford, she combined her interest in writing and the theatre: her plays *You've No Need to Be Frightened* and *Having a Wonderful Time* were staged as student productions. In 1958, her play *Downstairs* won first prize at the National Student Drama Festival. While still at university, Churchill had a vision of the provocative possibilities offered by the playwriting process, writing: 'We need to find new questions which may help us answer the old ones or make them unimportant and this means new subjects and new forms.'[7] Churchill's dedication to continually questioning the status quo and discovering new subjects and forms has not wavered over the decades.

A degree from Oxford was an established way of entering London's professional playwriting profession, but Churchill took a circuitous path to the stage.[8] In 1961, she married the barrister David Harter, with whom she raised three boys. Churchill later articulated her personal struggle to balance the pull of writing with being actively involved with her children. Although she could afford a nanny, she felt conflicted 'about paying someone else to take care of *my* children, about the feeling that I could do it better', while also feeling 'guilty if I did not accomplish something while I was paying someone else to baby-sit'. A key question that Churchill faced while setting her own priorities was: 'Are plays more important than raising kids?'[9] She decided to act as the primary caretaker of her sons and write during any spare time.

Although the 1960s were a period of rapid upheaval and change, Churchill's parental duties separated her from the era's events. However, Churchill reflected that her frustrations with the domestic sphere served to interest her in politics:

> I didn't feel a part of what was happening in the sixties. During that time I felt isolated. I had small children and was having miscarriages. It was an extremely solitary life. What politicized me was being discontent with my own life of being a barrister's wife and just being at home . . . It seemed claustrophobic. Having started off with undefined idealistic assumptions about the kind of life we could lead, we had drifted into something quite conventional and middle class and boring. By the mid-60s, I had this gloomy feeling that when the Revolution came I would be swept away.[10]

Despite time constraints, during this period Churchill wrote numerous radio plays for the BBC, starting with *The Ants* in 1962. Writing one-act plays for the radio allowed her more flexibility to spend time raising her sons. She had grown up listening to the radio and the genre utilized her concise ear for dialogue. *The Judge's Wife* (1972) was her first work for television, for which she later wrote *The Legion Hall Bombing* (1979).

While the 1960s were a frustrating decade for Churchill, during the 1970s she found communities of like-minded artists, and her entry into the London writing world resonates with the 1970s feminist slogan 'the personal is political'.[11] Thus Churchill looked back on the writing process of *Owners* as influenced by personal pain: 'I wrote it in three days. I'd just come out of hospital after a particularly gruesome late miscarriage. Still quite groggy and my arm ached because they'd given me an injection that didn't work. Into it [the play] went for the first time a lot of things that had been building up in me over a long time, political attitudes as well as personal ones.'[12] Churchill set *Owners* in Islington, a London suburb where she has lived since the 1960s. The play reflects the gentrification that had displaced some of the area's poorer residents. Churchill recalled that she became motivated by her research into the area's poor housing facilities, which coincided with her husband's career shift away from private practice into working for a legal aid group.[13] In *Owners*, Marion, the selfish real-estate developer, can be seen as a study for the central character Marlene in *Top Girls*.

In 1972 *Owners* premiered at the Royal Court, regarded as London's premiere venue for new playwrights. Since the foundation of the English Stage Company in 1956, the Royal Court Theatre had been associated with politically leftist playwrights. Particularly with the 1965 production of Edward Bond's *Saved*, the theatre became instrumental in the fight against censorship. From 1974–5 Churchill was the first female resident dramatist at the

Royal Court, where she also served as tutor for the Young Writers Group. Critics have compared Churchill's works to other feminist playwrights such as Sarah Daniels and Timberlake Wertenbaker, both of whom contributed notable works to the Royal Court's stages during the 1980s: Wertenbaker gained popular and critical success with *Our Country's Good* while Daniels' *Masterpieces* provoked controversy for its examination of sexism and pornography. More recently, Churchill's minimalist style has drawn comparisons to Harold Pinter and Samuel Beckett. (Churchill's presence has remained evident at the Royal Court Theatre through productions of new works as well as revivals, such as a series of her one-act radio plays which she directed in 2002.)

During the 1970s, Churchill became involved in political and experimental theatre groups, and in 1974, she wrote *Objections to Sex and Violence*, which some critics consider her first explicitly feminist work. The play depicts two bourgeois sisters, one of whom rebels to become a political terrorist. Reflecting on her evolving relationship to feminism, Churchill commented: 'For years and years I thought of myself as a writer before I thought of myself as a woman, but recently I've found that I would say I was a feminist writer as opposed to other people saying I was.'[14] Her feminist awakening corresponded to her work's prioritization of women's issues. Churchill states that she had initially felt that as a 'woman writer' she needed to portray male protagonists to prove herself, but that now she wanted to give women characters the 'knotty problem(s)'.[15] *Top Girls'* examination of the tensions between motherhood and career clearly illustrates this decision to explore women's issues.

The year 1976 marked a turning point for Churchill's work and political outlook, when she met members of the feminist theatre group Monstrous Regiment, which had been founded the year before to provide the opportunities for women that were lacking in both mainstream and fringe theatres. The group's name stems from a sixteenth-century pamphlet by John Knox entitled 'The first blast of the trumpet against the monstrous regiment of women'.[16] As befits their name, the group worked with Churchill to address prejudices towards unorthodox women. Churchill collaborated with Monstrous Regiment on *Vinegar Tom*, an examination of the witch-hunts of the seventeenth century that depicted the so-called witches as societal scapegoats. Churchill credits Monstrous Regiment members for encouraging her analytical focus, recalling discussions with group members about the roles of women and the economic pressures that instigated witch-hunts.[17] Instead of portraying the witch-hunts as a distant event, the production interrupted the historical narrative with aggressively contemporary songs, which related the past and present. Churchill collaborated with the group again on *Floorshow*, a cabaret that attempted to reverse the sexism usually associated with that genre.[18]

The year 1976 also initiated the beginning of her long working relationship with the director Max Stafford-Clark, with their production of *Light Shining in Buckinghamshire*. Her collaborations with Stafford-Clark and the Joint Stock collective are especially notable for their experimentations with form and multiple-role casting. For instance, in *Light Shining in Buckinghamshire* alternating actors portrayed feuding characters during the English Revolution. Through this pioneering technique, the company represented the era's population, with the actors' process of working together creating a sense of community. Since the audience cannot necessarily keep all of the characters distinct, the play avoided emphasizing an individual's journey, choosing to foreground the ways in which rapid upheaval affects community members from all social strata. Instead of one actor representing a singular point of view, each actor had to walk in multiple characters' shoes. This process opened up possibilities for audience members to construct their own comparisons and contrasts between different characters' situations and perspectives. Churchill has continued to work with

Stafford-Clark throughout his tenure as Artistic Director of the Royal Court and, since 1993, with his Out of Joint Theatre Company.

Cloud Nine in 1979 was Churchill's first hit, transferring to New York and winning her first Obie Award. Developed with Joint Stock members, the actors were chosen to represent diverse views on sexual and gender identities, and Churchill integrated their personal experiences into the script. She experimented with shifting time and locales, setting the first half of the play in a British colony in Africa during the Victorian era and the second half in London in 1979, but as if only 25 years had apparently passed for the characters. Churchill furthered her experiments in casting, with *Cloud Nine*'s cross-gender and racial casting purposefully demonstrating the effects of patriarchy and imperialism. In the one-act play *Three More Sleepless Nights* (1980) she experimented with the overlapping dialogue technique that she was soon to develop further in *Top Girls*.

Following *Top Girls*, Churchill continued to critique capitalism, portraying the disparity between 'the haves' and 'have nots'. Produced only months after *Top Girls*, *Fen* has been referred to as 'Bottom Girls' and 'Land Girls'.[19] The Fen women extend Churchill's depictions of disenfranchised and immobilized women. Produced with Joint Stock, the play won Churchill her first Susan Smith Blackburn Prize for drama. The verse drama *Serious Money* (1987), Churchill's depiction of London's financial traders, was so biting that British Telecom notoriously refused to let its telephones be used in the production, in order to avoid being associated with the play's politics.[20] However, the production's energy ended up having the reverse effect than that intended, with many of the trader types that it satirized embracing the play, making it Churchill's biggest hit. *Serious Money* became her first play to transfer to Broadway, winning numerous prizes along the way, including an Olivier Award. Churchill's ongoing critique of institutions that determine 'normal' behaviour found its most evident expression in *Softcops*. She wrote the first draft of the play in 1978, although the Royal Shakespeare Company first performed the play in 1984 at the Barbican Theatre. While *Top Girls* explores career women's pursuit of power and money during the contemporary moment, *Softcops* has an all-male cast and looks back to methods of control first established during the 1830s. The play's depiction of power relations was deeply influenced by theories articulated in Michel Foucault's *Discipline and Punish*.

In *Top Girls*, Churchill explored the complexities of mother-hood, a theme that can be traced throughout her body of work. In 1994, *The Skriker* premiered at the National Theatre. The play's plot focuses on two teenage mothers: a young mother who has killed her baby and been confined to a mental hospital, and another pregnant runaway. While *The Skriker* depicts a world that is inhospitable to young mothers, *A Number* (2002) depicts a world devoid of mothering, and explores the chilling ramifica-tions of cloning. In *Blue Kettle*, a so-called long-lost son attempts to fool various mothers who had once given their sons up for adoption.

Churchill's constant exploration of style has enabled her to move smoothly between the political style frequently associated with an older generation of playwrights, and the minimalist ten-dencies of newer playwrights. Thus, Churchill is one of a select group of playwrights to have successfully bridged the generation gap, with emerging playwrights considering her work to be a con-tinuing influence.[21] Stafford-Clark reflected that Churchill's growing recognition as a writer meant she could 'write the rulebook' (2007, p. 105). Churchill's criteria changes each time she writes a play, and she sees her works' content and form as interlinked: 'I enjoy finding the form that seems to best fit what I'm thinking about . . . on the whole I enjoy plays that are non-naturalistic and don't move at real time.'[22] Accordingly, and in contrast to the majority of mainstream British theatre, she has increasingly favoured non-realistic styles.

The abstraction and minimalism of Churchill's recent works continue to test the boundaries of theatre, while provocatively allowing for various interpretations. For example, in each scene of *This Is a Chair* (1997), Churchill presents a heading of a contemporary political topic while simultaneously depicting a seemingly unrelated domestic conflict, inducing the audience to make their own connections. *Blue Heart* (2000) consists of two one-act plays: in *Heart's Desire*, continuous repetition postpones a potential reunion between a travelling daughter and her family. Churchill challenges the fixity of identity when, for example, the daughter enters, but as a giant bird. In *Blue Kettle*, Churchill increasingly replaces the words 'blue' and 'kettle' with other apparently random words, emphasizing the malleability of memory and the arbitrariness of language. Additionally, Churchill has shown an increasing tendency to mix genres, as illustrated by her collaborations with the dance company Second Stride on *Lives of the Great Poisoners* (1991) and *Hotel* (1997). Fellow artists frequently cite Churchill's continual process of reinvention as one of her most esteemed qualities.[23]

Churchill was motivated to write *Top Girls* partially through her understanding of British political differences with the USA; and the depiction of Anglo-American relations continues as a thread in her work. In *Icecream* (1989), she strikes a darkly humorous chord with her depiction of American tourists who travel to Britain to reclaim their roots, only to discover criminal relatives who subvert their nostalgic expectations. In 2003, Churchill compiled documentary material for a staged reading entitled 'Iraq.doc'. Although she wrote *Far Away* (2000) before 9/11, reviewers have related the play to the ongoing Middle East conflict. The play depicts a world of shifting loyalties, in which characters consider as enemies not only the citizens of other nations, but children, animals and plants.

While in *Far Away* Churchill achieves her political points through innuendo, her most recent work *Drunk Enough to Say I Love You?* (2006) refers directly to recent news events. The two characters, with names that are ever so thinly veiled references to the Union Jack and Uncle Sam, are portrayed as political collaborators and (more daringly) as gay lovers. The relationship drew comparisons to George W. Bush and Tony Blair and synthesized the overt politicism of Churchill's previous works with her recent minimalism.

Social, political and historical background

Churchill wrote *Top Girls* as a direct response to political events, and understanding the play's historical moment will contextualize its arguments. While the election of Margaret Thatcher as Britain's first female prime minister could be seen as a victory for equal representation, Churchill wrote *Top Girls* in opposition to Thatcherism. Having become politicized during the 1970s, Churchill saw the 1980s shift from a socialist mindset to a capitalist emphasis as an ominous change. This difference became particularly clear to her when comparing British and US concepts of female equality. This section examines different types of feminisms, and begins by outlining important moments in the 1970s feminist movement and highlighting differences between US and British views. It goes on to provide some background on socialist concepts of class conflict, and closes with an outline of Thatcher's right-wing policies.

Different types of feminisms

The women's liberation movement of the 1970s focused on uniting women as 'sisters' and on politicizing women according to the slogan 'the personal is political'. The movement is often termed 'second-wave feminism', with the suffragette movement of the early twentieth century comprising the first wave. In 1970 Ruskin College, Oxford, hosted a women's conference that illustrated both the changes that had already occurred, and hopes for further reforms. Oxford University had been the alma mater of both Churchill and Margaret Thatcher, whose opposing political influences and viewpoints will be the focus of this chapter. However, until 1963 neither woman would have been allowed to join the Oxford Union, which is where the women conference attendees now pitched their tents. Many of this generation of women had been involved in protests against Vietnam and wanted to take revolutionary goals further, breaking with the traditionally domestic role of women. The women made a series of demands that became foundational to the 1970s Women's Liberation movement: equal pay, equal education and opportunity, 24-hour nurseries, free contraception and abortion on demand.[24] Second-wave feminists intended these goals to be the starting point for achieving far-ranging equal rights.

The movement became more public when the so-called 'women libbers' demonstrated at the Miss World contest of 1970, and soon after staged their first large march in London. By protesting against the sexist beauty standards of beauty contests, the British feminists were joining their US counterparts, who in 1968 had famously protested at the Miss America Pageant. Later derided as 'bra burners', the women took objects that they felt symbolized women's oppression – bras, girdles, high-heeled shoes, *Playboy* and women's magazines – and threw them into a rubbish bin.[25] These acts had an evident theatrical air, and feminist performance groups became an effective part of street demonstrations. In England, feminist groups such as the Women's Theatre Group and Monstrous Regiment organized ongoing groups and performed pieces that could stand on their own as forms of protest. Plays such as the Women's Theatre Group's *My Mother Says I Never Should* (1975), about teenage sexuality, also toured schools, in an effort to offer progressive education.[26] Political reformers saw performance as a way to challenge dominant culture, and Churchill was engaging in collaborative ways of writing with both socialist and feminist theatre groups formed during the 1970s.

Churchill recalls that her initial motivation to write *Top Girls* stemmed from confronting different understandings of feminism:

> When I was in the States in '79 I talked to some women who were saying how well things were going for women in America now with far more top executives being women, and I was struck by the difference between that and the feminism I was used to in England which is far more closely connected with socialism.[27]

In order to understand *Top Girls'* political implications, it is useful to keep in mind that although it is common to refer to feminism as a unified movement, there are in fact many kinds. Churchill wrote *Top Girls* at a time when these feminisms were at a crucial point, and her play provided a timely critique of the bourgeois feminist trends that were especially prominent in the USA. Elaine Aston recalls that *Top Girls'* first staging in 1982 diverged from 1970s feminist politics of sisterhood because it was a play based on a 'politics of difference' (2001, p. 38). By recognizing the socioeconomic differences between women, the play encouraged a re-examination of feminist priorities.

Although there are many different types of feminism, we will address three main groupings: radical feminism, bourgeois feminism and materialist feminism. Similar to many minority groups, feminist groups have faced the ongoing dilemma of choosing between remaining separate from dominant culture in order to establish a shared sense of identity, and wanting to integrate. Radical feminists support separation from male-dominated culture, emphasizing women's unique and superior characteristics. In contrast, bourgeois feminists seek equality with men within existing social structures, and minimize the differences between the genders. Both feminisms focus on the individual, which differentiates them from socialist feminism's emphasis on the group.[28]

Churchill considers herself a socialist feminist, which is also often referred to as materialist feminism, stemming from Karl Marx's focus on economic relationships. The feminist theatre scholar Sue-Ellen Case explains what differentiates materialist feminism from other feminisms:

> Rather than assuming that the experiences of women are induced by gender oppression from men or that liberation can be brought about by virtue of women's unique gender strengths, that patriarchy is everywhere and always the same and that all women are 'sisters', the materialist position underscores the role of class and history in creating the oppression of women ... Not only are all women not sisters, but women in the privileged class actually oppress women in the working class. (1988, pp. 82–3)

Case's description particularly parallels Churchill's examination of sisterhood, with Margaret Thatcher and Marlene in *Top Girls* both being rejected as 'sisters'. Although both women could be seen as having achieved success from a bourgeois feminist perspective, they engage in 'intra' gender oppression of their working-class counterparts.

US and British branches of feminism developed differently, resulting in British feminists being more sympathetic to socialism while Americans assumed a more bourgeois perspective.[29] Many American feminists had been involved in the Civil Rights and anti-war movements during the 1960s, and viewed feminism as a companion to these struggles. However, the US emphasis on bourgeois concerns led to the movement being criticized for ignoring the concerns of blue-collar workers and minority women.[30] While identifying as a socialist in the USA often bore a stigma because of the Cold War antagonism against any form of 'Reds', women in

Britain were more likely to associate themselves with socialism and be aware of class solidarity and conflict. British feminists tended to take economic factors into consideration, seeing state-supported social services as playing a necessary role in national life. Furthermore, during the 1970s trade unions were markedly more powerful in Britain than in the USA. Therefore, British socialist feminists were more likely to attempt to see their feminist goals as compatible with union demands and to try to work with their union 'brothers' and 'sisters' to enact social change.[31] However, they found that they were underrepresented in labour hierarchies and struggled with the sexism of many male members of the left.[32]

There were different outcomes to the women's liberation movements in both countries. The US founding of NOW (the National Organization of Women) in 1966 has no direct counterpart in Britain. However, the US women's right to choose, established in the landmark decision of Roe versus Wade (1973), continues to be attacked by right-wing Christianity, which has a more fervent following in the USA than in Britain. Moreover, British efforts towards legislative reform were generally more successful, with the Equal Pay Act passing in 1970 and instituted in 1975;[33] while the year that *Top Girls* premiered, the Equal Rights Amendment was defeated in the USA after an extended political struggle.[34]

Of course, equal rights legislation is only as effective as its implementation. A mid-1980s survey of British employers revealed that many were avoiding or unaware of the implications of passed equal pay and opportunities legislation.[35] By 1988, women in Britain still made up only 6 per cent of directors and 10 per cent of senior managers.[36] Although the visibility of women in high-powered positions increased in both countries during the 1980s, the 'glass ceiling' remained daunting.

Socialism

Churchill sees feminism and socialism as intimately conjoined, reflecting: 'I do find it hard to conceive of a right-wing feminism. Of course, socialism and feminism aren't synonymous, but I feel strongly about both and wouldn't be interested in a form of one that didn't include the other.'[37] *Top Girls* builds to a debate between 'us' and 'them' that harks back to Marxist concepts regarding class structure. In *The Communist Manifesto*, Karl Marx and Friedrich Engels depict their view of class struggle: 'Our epoch . . . possesses . . . this distinctive feature: it has simplified the class antagonisms. Society as a whole is more and more splitting up into two great hostile camps, into two great classes directly facing each other – bourgeoisie and proletariat' (1935, p. 23). Without successful class uprising, Marx identifies the proletariat's condition as dehumanizing, since it is continually at the mercy of the Capitalist system. He defines the proletariat as:

> a class of labourers, who live only so long as they find work, and who find work only so long as their labour increases capital. These labourers, who must sell themselves piecemeal, are a commodity . . . and are consequently exposed to . . . all the fluctuations of the market. (1935, p. 30)

Therefore, from a Marxist perspective, 'us' refers to those who are economically downtrodden, and 'them' to the members of the upper classes who profit off the labour of the masses. This conflict has been represented in various theatrical incarnations by many of Churchill's left-minded colleagues, and she builds upon these precedents.

While *Top Girls* was first produced at the beginning of the 1980s, it foresees the class antagonisms that characterized the decade. The 1984 Miners' Strike crystallized the class distinctions between 'us' vs 'them', polarizing supporters of the left against

Thatcher's government. The socialist feminist historian Sheila Rowbotham pinpoints the strike as a turning point in labour relations: 'No mere strike, this became a contest with a government that wanted to break a key section of the labour movement . . . (with) exceptional circumstances of violent pickets, roadblocks, phone-tapping and villages surrounded and invaded by police' (1997, p. 484). Despite holding out throughout a long, arduous struggle, the miners eventually faced defeat. The outcome signified a weakening of the union's bargaining power and a corresponding strengthening of the government's anti-labour policies.

Thatcherism

In addition to being influenced by her socialist politics, Churchill recalls that the play was also closely linked to Thatcher's recent rise to power:

> Thatcher had just become prime minister; there was talk about whether it was an advance to have a woman prime minister if it was someone with policies like hers: She may be a woman but she isn't a sister, she may be a sister but she isn't a comrade. And, in fact, things have got much worse for women under Thatcher.[38]

Following Thatcher's election, the media touted her personal biography to illustrate the powerful positions that women could achieve through personal initiative. Rowbotham describes Thatcher's view of feminism:

> The fact that a woman could become Prime Minister had a symbolic meaning; modern women, it seemed, could do anything now. However, like many of her generation, Margaret Thatcher, born in 1925, did not want to be seen as a woman in politics. She preferred to be a politician who happened to be a

woman and she had little sympathy with the post-war generation's preoccupation with women's right and wrongs. (1997, p.
472)

Thatcher's father was a grocer, and so her class background as well
as her gender made her an outsider to the political establishment.
She attended Oxford University, became a tax lawyer, and worked
her way up through the political ranks. Thatcher, like Marlene in
Top Girls, found it necessary to leave class markers behind her,
taking elocution lessons during college.[39] As prime minister, she
spoke in an upper-class accent and adopted the royal 'we' on
occasion. For her steadfast attitude, Thatcher gained the nickname
'The Iron Lady', and later, 'TINA', for her repeated assertion
'There Is No Alternative'.[40] A charismatic politician and personality, Thatcher was opposed to the tradition of finding consensus in
British politics. She inspired strong feelings in the British public,
with people either loving or hating her.[41]

Thatcher and fellow New Right politicians believed in monetarism – trying to control the money supply and inflation and
considering market forces to be the primary way to restore the
economy. They emphasized individual initiative and minimized
government involvement in economic matters, making drastic cuts
in public programmes.[42] The budget cuts functioned to disband
the Welfare State, which had been set up as part of Britain's
economic recovery from the Second World War. Thatcher also
pursued the privatization, or selling off, of nationally owned utili-
ties such as British Gas, Britoil, water and electricity: she was
strongly opposed to such socialist elements in British government,
viewing private ownership as more efficient.[43]

Thatcher's spending cuts were particularly hard on education
and the arts, with the result that many of the theatre groups formed
during the 1970s struggled or disbanded, including Monstrous
Regiment. Additionally, Thatcherism increased state control by

increasing the security forces and taking power away from local governments. By doing so, she was able eventually to emerge victorious in the long power struggle between the central government and the unions.

The 1980s became a time when women had a figurehead of power in Margaret Thatcher, but no guarantee of equal opportunity. The so-called 'me' decade of the 1980s soon challenged the 1970s ideals of 'sisterhood'. The 'new woman' or 'working woman' was meant to aspire towards the career ladder, pursuing an ethic of individualism. While women who were able to enter well-paid professions, start their own businesses, or buy property could do well in the 1980s, their lower-paid counterparts had increasingly less security.[44] Britain's unemployment figures more than doubled between Thatcher's election and the play's premiere, reaching over three million, which represented more than 11 per cent of the population.[45] Thatcherite policies affected low-income mothers in immediate ways, with cuts in maternity provisions and ending of free school meals.[46] During the 1980s, working mothers had increasingly to fit their family responsibilities around multiple part-time jobs.[47] Tax cuts were unequally distributed; for instance, in Thatcher's inaugural budget of 1979, the richest 7 per cent received 34 per cent of the total tax cuts, while the poorest 10 per cent received only 2 per cent.[48]

As well as mounting economic disparity, there was also an evidently growing geographical division. While London became increasingly prosperous during the 1980s, the North was in an increasing state of decline and unemployment, partially due to a sharp decline in manufacturing jobs.[49] These deepening conflicts are reflected by polls: between 1983 and 1986 the percentage of people who recorded 'great' or 'quite a lot' of confidence in the government had dropped from 54 per cent to 10 per cent.[50]

Although Churchill was motivated primarily by Thatcher's rise to power, she also references President Reagan's policies. US voters first elected Reagan in 1980, and he became Thatcher's most important political ally. 'Reaganomics' had many similarities with Thatcherism, particularly in the emphasis on the market and on tax cuts for the upper income brackets. Like Thatcher, Reagan had a defining showdown with a union, defeating the air traffic controller's strike in 1981.[51] Churchill particularly references Reagan's stance against Communism, which went back to his days as an actor when he had been a 'friendly witness', supporting Joseph McCarthy's House of Un-American Activities.[52]

Throughout the 1980s, the USA and USSR vied for the upper hand as competing super powers. Thatcher's support of Reagan's international policy led to controversial decisions such as allowing the housing of US cruise missiles on British soil. The year before *Top Girls* premiered, a group of 30 peace protesters, most of them women with small children, marched approximately 120 miles from Cardiff to the military base at Greenham. Here the women remained setting up camp, with some chaining themselves to the gates in protest. Although the women received an outpouring of public support, the missiles remained, and in 1984 police cleared the peace camp.[53]

2 Analysis and Commentary

This chapter is a full-length study of *Top Girls*, focusing on the play as a literary text. The play has an untraditional plot line, so the opening plot summary provides a helpful outline of the basic action. The accompanying character analysis section synthesizes key information on all of the play's figures. The chapter then examines the origins of the play, and its theatrical influences and styles. There follows close readings of several important scenes from the play, paying attention to Churchill's word choice and overarching themes. Finally, this chapter analyses the scholarly response to the play's political ramifications and innovations in form.

Plot summary

Act One
Top Girls opens in a restaurant where the main character, Marlene, is hosting a dinner party. Marlene is a career woman during the early 1980s, and has recently received a promotion to managing director. However, the five characters whom she invites to her celebration are not from her era, but are either historical figures or fictional characters from literature and art. The first to arrive are Isabella Bird and Lady Nijo, two real historical figures who became known through their published writings. Pope Joan and Dull Gret arrive soon afterwards. Pope Joan is debatably a real-life or mythical figure: a woman from the ninth century who cross-dressed so convincingly that she reportedly became Pope. In contrast to the

historical figures who are known through their public roles, Dull Gret is a fictional character depicted in a painting by Brueghel.

The characters talk over each other, discussing their love lives, travels and families. Marlene proposes a toast, remarking on how far they have come, and the rest of the characters toast her accomplishment in return.

The mood switches as Pope Joan continues her story. She reveals that she lived as a man from the age of 12 in order to continue her education. She eventually rose through the church establishment and became Pope. Meanwhile, she also had an affair with one of her chamberlains, and became pregnant. She gave birth to the child unexpectedly during a procession and, exposed as a woman, she was stoned to death.

While Joan tells her story Nijo interjects and talks about her four children. Her first baby was the Emperor's son, but the infant died. Nijo had to hide her next pregnancies because they resulted from her affairs, and her lovers took the infants away from her. She had her fourth baby in the hills and stayed away from everyone, but she no longer felt anything for the infant. Marlene wonders why, in contrast to the joyful celebration she had planned, they are so miserable.

The final guest to arrive is the tardy Patient Griselda, a fictional character from Geoffrey Chaucer's *The Canterbury Tales*. Griselda tells her story and it becomes clear that, unlike the other characters, she has no voice of her own. Although she was born to a peasant family, a marquis unexpectedly selected her as his wife. However, the condition of her marriage was that she had to obey her husband Walter without question. Griselda agreed and always adhered to her promise, no matter what extreme sacrifices he asked of her. Walter insisted on having her two infants taken away from her and apparently killed. He told her it was because the peasant people were discontent with him having children who were partially of peasant stock. However, she believed that Walter really needed to have proof that she loved him. Finally, her husband decided to send Griselda back to her father, with nothing but a slip as clothing. Walter tested her again by asking her to help prepare his wedding to a new, younger wife. After Griselda assisted the girl getting ready, Walter revealed that the young woman was actually their daughter. Griselda found out that Walter had secretly allowed both their son and daughter to grow up. Made content by his wife's unquestioning obedience, Walter took Griselda back, finally reuniting the family.

Marlene expresses her frustration over Griselda's acquiescence to her husband's requirements. Nijo is also upset, because unlike Griselda, nobody had returned her children to her. Nijo does remember how one time she beat the emperor for a perceived injustice. Gret, who has remained mostly silent throughout the meal, tells her story, recalling how she and other women journeyed through hell and beat the devils. Isabella talks about the last trip that she took, where she was the first European woman to meet the Emperor of Morocco. By this time, the women have become consistently drunker, and arguably sadder and more estranged, with Pope Joan lapsing into Latin and then vomiting.

Act Two Scene 1

The second act opens in Marlene's office at the *Top Girls* Employment Agency in London. Marlene is in the process of interviewing a young woman, Jeanine, in order to find her a job placement. Marlene instructs the newly engaged Jeanine that she should not tell her potential employers that she is getting married, because they will assume that she will leave her job to have children. Although Jeanine has a vague idea of wanting to travel, Marlene evaluates Jeanine's potential and suggests some low-level local jobs. Marlene insists that she is risking her reputation by giving her recommendation, and Jeanine agrees that she will do her best to get a job at a lampshade company.

Act Two Scene 2

The play shifts to an evening in Joyce's backyard in Suffolk. Joyce is Marlene's sister, who still lives in the working-class community in which they grew up. Joyce's 16-year-old daughter, Angie, and her 12-year-old friend Kit are talking in a shelter built in Joyce's backyard. Joyce repeatedly calls Angie, but Angie and Kit both ignore her. Angie tells Kit that she wants to kill her mother and have Kit watch. Kit is worried about a nuclear war and insists that they should move to New Zealand in case of a bombing. Angie reveals her big secret: that she is going to go to London and visit her aunt Marlene, whom she believes is actually her mother.

Angie and Kit had planned to go to the cinema, but Joyce insists that Angie needs to clean her room before she can go. Angie leaves and Joyce and Kit talk about the two girls' plans for the future. While Angie has left school, the clever Kit wants to be a nuclear physicist. Angie goes to her room and returns dressed up in her fancy blue dress, which is too small for her. Joyce gets increasingly angry at Angie's refusal to clean her room. It begins to rain and Joyce and Kit retreat inside. When Kit comes back outside to get Angie, Angie reveals that she put the dress on to kill her mother.

Act Two Scene 3

It is Monday morning again at the *Top Girls* Agency where Marlene's co-workers, Win and Nell, are gossiping. Win chats to Nell about the affair that she is having with a married man, revealing that she spent the weekend at his house while his wife was out of town. They contemplate switching jobs, because Marlene has recently been promoted over them and this might limit their prospects: they can have no further possible aspirations with the firm since there can be only one Top Girl. However, they tell Marlene that they are glad that she got the promotion over the runner-up candidate, Howard Kidd.

Win interviews Louise, a 46-year-old woman who has been in the same job for 21 years. Louise tells Win that she had not feel appreciated at her previous company since her bosses passed her over for promotion, and because she even trained others who were promoted over her. Win believes that her potential will be limited due to the younger men who will be her competition, but finds a cosmetic company that might hire her. When Louise discusses her frustrations with her old workplace, Win reprimands her by saying that she should not talk so much at an interview.

Next, Angie arrives at the office, having travelled to London to see her aunt. Marlene asks Angie if Joyce knows where she is, but receives an indefinite answer. Angie becomes distraught when Marlene does not seem to want Angie to stay at her apartment.

Howard's wife, Mrs Kidd, interrupts their conversation when she enters the office and insists on talking to Marlene. Mrs Kidd explains how upset she and Howard feel about a woman being promoted over him, and hopes that Marlene will turn down the offer so the bosses will promote him instead. Marlene, however, is dismissive. After she leaves, Angie (who overhead the conversation) tells Marlene that she thinks her attitude was admirable.

Nell then interviews Shona, who claims that she is 29 and describes her successful life on the road as a saleswoman. However, by the end of the interview it is clear to Nell that Shona has been making up her credentials. She admits that she is actually only 21, and has no real work experience. Meanwhile, Marlene has left Angie in the office while she works away from her desk. Angie tells Win that she wants to work at the agency, but she has no credentials. Win starts to tell Angie her life story, but Angie falls asleep. Nell enters and informs Win that Howard has had a heart attack. Marlene returns to the office and Win tells her that Angie wants to work at the agency. However, Marlene responds that Angie has severely limited prospects.

Act Three

This act is chronologically the earliest, taking place on a Sunday afternoon in Joyce's kitchen a year before the rest of the play. The act starts with Angie opening the presents that Marlene has bought for Joyce and Angie. Angie unwraps the blue dress that she wore in the earlier backyard scene. She joyfully tries the dress on, which fits her at that time.

Meanwhile, it becomes clear that Angie has manipulated the sisters into meeting by misleadingly telling Marlene that Joyce wanted her to visit. The two women scold Angie for deceiving them, but she reminds them that the last time her aunt visited was for her ninth birthday. Joyce admits that her husband left three years before. Joyce sends Angie to bed and Marlene plans to sleep on the couch.

In private, the sisters argue about their childhoods, different life choices and politics. While Marlene blames their alcoholic father for abusing their mother, Joyce sees him as having had an oppressed life as well. When Marlene accuses Joyce of being jealous of her career, Joyce criticizes Marlene for deserting her family. In the course of the argument, it is revealed that Angie is Marlene's biological daughter: Marlene got pregnant at 17 and left her baby with her elder sister to raise. Marlene offers Joyce money to help, but Joyce refuses. While Marlene praises Thatcher's policies, Joyce expresses class resentment. As Marlene is trying to fall asleep on the couch, Angie walks in having woken from a nightmare. The play ends with her word: 'Frightening' (141).

Character analysis

The dinner party

Marlene

Marlene is a successful London businesswoman, who has recently been promoted to the managing director of Top Girls Employment

Agency. She has previously worked in the USA and appears to lead a glamorous life. However, Marlene has focused on her career to the exclusion of her personal relationships, leaving her biological daughter to be raised by her elder sister. She has minimal contact with her family and does not discuss them with her co-workers.

Marlene believes that she has escaped her working-class background, and blames her past for the emptiness in her life. While she has an imaginary community of women friends, she does not seem to have any real-life friends with whom to celebrate. She has sexual relationships with men, but notes that they cannot handle a long-term relationship with such a 'high flying' career woman. Since giving birth to Angie, she has had two abortions and thinks she has been on the Pill for so long that she is probably sterile. She does not show concern for Angie when she comes to visit, instead carrying on with her work.

Isabella Bird

Isabella is the first of Marlene's dinner guests to arrive, and she is the most talkative of the group. She is based on a Scottish woman who lived from 1831 to 1904 and became known for her travel writings. Born the daughter of a clergyman, Isabella had a very adventurous life for a woman of her era, and never had children. During her travels, she kept in contact with her sister Hennie, who she regards as the good, proper sister. At 50 years old, she married her sister's doctor.

Although she suffered from illness, Isabella travelled extensively later in life. When she returned to Scotland, she would engage in charitable activities to atone for having led a life based on self-satisfaction.

Gret

Dull Gret is the subject of a painting by Brueghel titled 'Dulle Griet'. The picture portrays her in an apron and armour, leading a group of women into hell to battle with devils. Unlike the rest of the dinner guests, Gret is a peasant and a representative of the working class, and her language is rough in comparison to the quick banter of the rest of the guests. Partially due to this difference, Gret is quiet throughout the dinner, answering questions briefly and only when addressed directly. However, near the end of the scene, Gret makes the longest speech of the party, describing the wartime horror that motivated her to travel to hell and fight with the grotesque devils. She says the terror of the Spanish army was worse, and describes the violent deaths of two of her ten children.

Pope Joan

There is an ongoing controversy about whether Pope Joan existed. Believers insist that she was elected Pope in 854 and ruled successfully for two years. Considered a child prodigy, Joan lived as a man from the age of 12 in order to continue her education. She enjoyed the authority and extravagances of being Pope, as well as debating the finer points of religious philosophy. Joan reflects that church doctrine considered her a heretic and reveals that she never heard from God in the direct way that she expected. Although there were natural disasters during her time as Pope, she insists that she does not hold herself responsible. Joan's gender was revealed during a public procession in which she gave birth on the street. She recalls that she was stoned to death, and believes that her baby was also murdered.

Lady Nijo

Based on a woman who was born in 1258, Nijo was raised to be a courtesan to the Emperor of Japan. When she first had sex with the Emperor she cried throughout, but she does not consider herself to have been raped because she belonged to the Emperor. She reveals to Marlene that although she laughs frequently, she is not a cheerful person. However, she describes having a moment of rebellion against the Emperor: when he broke protocol by letting his attendants beat the women with sticks, she retaliated by beating him.

After being rejected from court apparently due to the Empress's jealousy, Nijo became a Buddhist nun and travelled throughout Japan on foot. She had to give up her children due to societal pressures.

Nijo is hyperaware of her clothes, which are symbolic of social status in the Japanese court. In particular, she wonders whether she would have been permitted to wear the appropriate robes to the Emperor's funeral. At the end of the meal, Nijo is distraught because her children were never returned to her.

Patient Griselda

The aptly named Patient Griselda was a character in the Clerk's Tale in Geoffrey Chaucer's *Canterbury Tales*. She had repeatedly to prove that she would obey her husband by giving up her children. However, she says she loved them when Walter returned them to her, and insists that the reunited family felt content. Because she had turned over responsibility, she does not express regret for her decisions – although by the end of the dinner she does wonder if Walter had to take her children and test her in such an extreme manner.

Waitress

The waitress is a silent character who nonetheless represents the working class during the dinner scene. While the rest of the women discuss their achievements, the waitress responds to their demands. Marlene treats her briskly and demands quick service.

Joyce's house

Angie

Even though at the beginning of the play the audience thinks that Angie is Joyce's child, Angie says that she suspects that she is secretly Marlene's daughter. Whether this is wishful thinking or intuition, she hits upon the truth.

Unlike her biological mother, Angie is not considered 'clever', being placed in remedial classes, and leaving school by 16 with no qualifications. Joyce and Marlene believe that her future is limited, envisioning her as staying home dependent on Joyce, having to get married or working as a packer at a grocery store. Angie expresses frustration with her life and resents Joyce, threatening violence towards her. In contrast, she admires Marlene's glamorous lifestyle and regards Marlene's brief visit as the best time in her life. Angie manages to trick the sisters into meeting and travels to London to meet with her 'aunt'.

Angie has a close companion in her neighbour Kit, who is four years younger than she is. Angie believes in extrasensory powers, wondering if she has the potential to move objects with her mind, and partakes in extreme rites of friendship, even tasting Kit's menstrual blood. Angie keeps a secret notebook, which Marlene reveals contains plans to take over the world.

Joyce

Joyce is Marlene's older sister and the woman who has raised Angie. Joyce decided to stay in the same area that she grew up in, and has remained loyal to her family and social class. She often visits her elderly mother and maintains her father's gravesite, even though he was abusive. She eventually told her unfaithful husband Frank to leave, and now thinks that she is better off without a man in her life. When Marlene unexpectedly became pregnant with Angie it seemed as though the already married Joyce might not be able to have children. Joyce unexpectedly became pregnant, but due to taking care of Angie, was not able to stay off her feet long enough to keep from miscarrying. Partially due to the miscarriage, Joyce resents both Angie and Marlene. When Angie ignores her calls to come in the house, she first offers her a biscuit and then calls Angie a 'fucking rotten little cunt' (91) and says that Angie can stay outside and die.

Although she struggles to support herself and Angie by holding down four cleaning jobs, Joyce refuses Marlene's offer of money and thinks that Marlene has betrayed her class by supporting Thatcher.

Kit

Kit is Angie's 12-year-old best friend who lives next door. While she has not been born into money, she represents the type of working-class girl who might be able to 'make it' as a result of Britain's changing economy during the 1980s. In contrast to Angie, she is clever, does well in school, and has career ambitions.

Although Kit plans to become a nuclear physicist, the ramifications of nuclear power frighten her. Fearing an imminent nuclear attack, she proposes travelling to New Zealand in order to be at the centre of the explosion, so that she will die quickly. She is not as impressed by Marlene as Angie is, and would rather have Angie go to the cinema with her than fight with Joyce. She expresses loyalty towards Angie, insisting that Joyce cannot stop them from being friends.

Office life

Mrs Kidd

As Howard's wife, Mrs Kidd is the sole character to be referred to only by her last name, as a reflection of her husband. She represents women from the previous generation who made their life choices before second-wave feminism occurred. Like many women of her generation, Mrs Kidd became a traditional domestic wife, depending on her husband for economic support. She insults Marlene and other career women who had more opportunities than she did, and views feminism as de-legitimizing her choices. Mrs Kidd is particularly emotional because her husband takes his career frustrations out on her, and she is extremely worried about her husband's fragile health.

Win

Win is one of Marlene's co-workers, who is well educated and was a high achiever at school, where she got a science degree. She is having an affair, and expresses excitement about sneaking around. When she tells Angie her life story, she reports that she travelled and was successful at sales, but drank when she was lonely. She also reveals that for a period of time she thought that she was insane and had split personalities, although the psychiatrist eventually gave her a clean bill of mental health.

Win was also married to a man who is now in prison, whom she does not visit often. She is more sympathetic than her co-workers are to the unfortunate, such as Howard and Angie. However, she responds harshly to Louise, perhaps threatened by the older career woman's story and not wanting to end up like her: Win downplays Louise's prospects and admonishes her not to talk at interviews so much.

Nell

Nell is another one of Marlene's co-workers at *Top Girls*. She is glad that Marlene got the promotion over Howard, but does not like coming in second. Nell implies that she might look for another job with better prospects. Her boyfriend Derek has asked her to marry him repeatedly, but she doubts that she will accept because her career is more important to her. Nell says that she was an excellent salesperson, although she is not very nice. Unlike Win, she expresses little sympathy when Howard has a heart attack, reflecting that it is just as well that he did not get the promotion.

Jeanine

The first character to be interviewed, Jeanine is a young woman seen by Marlene. She is currently a secretary, but fantasizes about being able to travel and have better prospects. She naively says that she is engaged, and Marlene implies that she should hide this fact from her employers, who will be concerned that she will get pregnant. Marlene tells her that she could have got higher qualifications, but Jeanine wanted to work right out of school, and she and her fiancé are saving money. Marlene convinces her that she is risking her own reputation by recommending her for the position, and persuades Jeanine to try to get the job. Ironically, however, the position offers her little improvement, being a clerical job at a lampshade establishment.

Louise

Win interviews Louise for a job placement, finding her to be at a disadvantage because of her age. Louise is 46, and has been stuck in middle management at the same firm for over 20 years. She believes that her superiors have repeatedly overlooked her for promotion, and do not appreciate her precise work. Louise reflects that she passes as a man at work and has sacrificed her social life. While she identifies her gender as having held her back in her career, she remains defensive towards women co-workers: she has tended to avoid mentoring women, and resents the new generation of women who takes their prospects for granted. Louise insists that she is willing to have a pay cut to leave her present job and hopes that her previous employers will regret their actions.

Shona

Nell interviews Shona for a placement. Shona tries to pass as a 'high flier', and initially Nell believes Shona's bravura and false resumé. However, when pressed for details of her life on the road, she recites a stream of lies that sound as though they come from advertisements. Shona does not express embarrassment for having lied, insisting that she could handle a high position if someone gave her the chance.

Influences and style

The origins of *Top Girls*

Churchill wrote the majority of the text of *Top Girls* between 1980 and 1982, although many of the ideas had been forming for years. Churchill describes the multiple strands of the play's development as follows:

> *Top Girls* is a play whose ideas came together over a period of time and in quite separate parts. Some years before I wrote it I'd had an idea for a play where a whole lot of people from the past, a whole lot of dead women came and had cups of coffee with someone who was alive now. That was just floating around as something quite sort of separate, by itself.

> Then I started thinking about a play possibly to do with women at work, and so I went and talked to quite lot of people doing different jobs. One of the places I visited was an employment agency, which later became a focus of the play. Then there was an idea of a play in which all the characters were women; the idea was to offer a huge range of different parts and give women the opportunity to play lots of roles on stage which they don't always get to play.

> At some point these various elements came together and I began to get the idea for a play about women at work, including women from the past, and a wide range of roles – and all of that fitted into the same play.[1]

As this quotation illustrates, Churchill combined historical and contemporary research with a feminist interest in providing actresses with quality roles. Although many critics have focused on Churchill's depiction of Marlene as a mother, Churchill reflects that the idea of Marlene being Angie's mother came late in the writing process.

Churchill saw her feminist and socialist messages as co-existing as dual layers of *Top Girls*:

> What I was intending to do was make it first look as though it was celebrating the achievements of women and then – by showing the main character, Marlene, being successful in a very competitive, destructive, capitalist way – ask, what kind of achievement is that? The idea was that it would start out looking like a feminist play and then turn into a socialist one, as well.[2]

To achieve this desired outcome, Churchill first presented a series of women from history to celebrate with Marlene. This decision would be interpreted as a feminist act because feminists during the 1970s often engaged in the reclaiming of female historical figures who were overlooked by mainstream scholars. Initially, some critics compared *Top Girls* to Judy Chicago's art piece *The Dinner Party* (1979), which had likewise portrayed a dinner table with places set for notable women from history, including Pope Joan.[3]

However, complicating the mainly positive view posited by other feminists' reclaiming of notable women is the fact that through the play's subsequent scenes, Churchill questions the merits of Marlene's achievement. Churchill concluded the play with a socialist argument that was familiar territory to many of her audience members: the common 'state of the nation' plays of the 1960s and 1970s, which explored British class conflicts, meant that Churchill could condense the concluding debate between Joyce and Marlene because her audience members would recognize her references.

Act One: source material

Instead of picking famous women, Churchill selected historical figures who would have been largely unknown to her audience members. Churchill acknowledged that she used *The Confessions of Lady Nijo* and *A Curious Life for a Lady: the Story of Isabella Bird* to help her develop her characters.

Lady Nijo lived during the Kamakura period and her memoirs detail her love life, including her fall from grace as Emperor GoFukakusa's concubine. While following a sedentary religious life after leaving the court was a socially acceptable alternative for upper-class women during her era, Nijo was exceptional for deciding to wander as a Buddhist nun among the common people.[4]

Nijo often expresses herself through romantic poetry, and also pays close attention to her garments, both characteristics that had rich symbolic meaning in courtly life.[5] Her life story had been lost to obscurity before scholars rediscovered and translated her writings in the mid-1960s.[6]

Isabella Bird became famous during the Victorian era for her books, which were based on her extensive travels. In one of Isabella's letters to her sister Hennie, she describes her relationship with 'Mountain man' Jim Nugent, whom she described as 'a man whom any woman might love but whom no sane woman would marry'[7] (one of the passages that Churchill uses in the play). Isabella's contemporaries remarked on the contrast between her hearty health while she travelled and the illnesses that plagued her when she attempted to live locally.[8]

Although Nijo and Isabella were known historical figures, whether Pope Joan really existed remains the subject of ongoing debate. Although Pope Clement VIII declared her a myth,[9] belief in her existence continues, based primarily on chronicles and artwork from the Middle Ages. Her believers point to the chair with a hole used in Vatican rituals and the detour taken by the

Papal procession to avoid the street where she was supposedly killed and buried.[10]

The legend surrounding the figure of Pope Joan remains powerful regardless of its veracity, and points to the allure of believing that a woman could usurp the highest position of patriarchal religious authority. At the close of the dinner scene, Joan quotes in Latin from *The Nature of Things* by Lucretius. The passage she selects focuses on the emotional distance made possible by intellectual pursuits within patriarchal institutions: 'nothing is sweeter than to sit in a quiet stronghold, fortified by the teaching of wise men and to be able to look down on others in their aimless wanderings.'[11]

Gret is unique not only because of her lower social class, but because she was inspired by the central image in Pieter the Elder Brueghel's 'Dulle Griet'(c. 1562). In her portrayal of Gret, Churchill can be seen as recuperating the character Dulle Griet, who is usually interpreted in a misogynistic manner as a manlike woman who could scare devils and escape from hell unharmed.[12] Griet has also been referred to as 'Mad Meg', and usually has been portrayed by art historians as covetous, instead of the revolutionary figure Churchill depicts.[13]

Churchill borrows the character of Griselda from Chaucer, Petrarch and Boccaccio, who portray her as a model of wifely patience. Griselda can be seen as representing the maiden characters who are saved by their princes in countless fairy tales. However, Churchill subverts her audience's expectations by illustrating the dark implications of such narratives. While her predecessors write from an omniscient viewpoint, letting the readers know that Griselda's children are being raised in secret,[14] Churchill relates the story from Griselda's perspective: the audience only becomes aware of her children's well-being when it is revealed to Griselda. This highlights Walter's cruelty and makes the audience question Griselda's loyal submission to her husband's patriarchal rule.

Joint Stock's influence

Joint Stock's methodology contributed to Churchill's willingness to experiment and collaborate. Founded in 1974, the theatre group was initially headed by Stafford-Clark as Artistic Director. Joint Stock productions tended to focus on communities of common people confronting times of change. Following their pivotal production of David Hare's *Fanshen*, depicting Chinese peasants turning to Communism, the company turned into a democratic collective.[15] The group nurtured collaborative methods of developing productions through a period of workshopping together, in which they researched the subject material, and explored attitudes towards the issues involved and the possible ways to show these. Churchill recalled that before working with Joint Stock, 'I'd never seen an exercise or improvisation before and I was as thrilled as a child at a pantomime.'[16] After the workshops, she would take time alone to write the play, and after she returned with a draft the rehearsal process would begin. This process tended to result in Stafford-Clark receiving parts of the scripts at different times and not having a finished play until close to the premiere. In contrast to the majority of theatre group experimentation with the collective writing process during the period, the Joint Stock method maintained the playwright's authority over the finished script.[17]

Although *Top Girls* was not a Joint Stock production, it shared the same director, numerous actors and casting techniques. Stafford-Clark favoured multiple-role casting because it gave company members more stage time, encouraged a tight-knit community and kept costs manageable. Additionally, Churchill had utilized multiple-role casting to political and theatrical effect in previous Joint Stock productions. In the case of *Top Girls*, Churchill recollects that she wrote the play without intending to cast actors in multiple roles, but Stafford-Clark proposed the casting choice.[18] This double and triple casting decided on in the first production has had a profound effect on the ways in which the audience members interpret the play. For example, the original production cross-cast Gret and Angie, both of whom are oppressed characters who are slow to speak, and deemed less intelligent than the others. The production also cross-cast Pope Joan and Louise, both of whom are characters who consider themselves to pass as men.

The director William Gaskill recalled that Joint Stock's working methods became a way to achieve Brechtian analysis,[19] which in turn influenced Churchill's writing style. When David Benedict asked Churchill why her works tended to veer away from a traditional focus on a central protagonist and linear narrative, Churchill responded that she considered her work with Joint Stock to have been a primary influence: 'When I was working with Joint Stock, I think there was a strong anti-sentimental feeling about in theatre. There was an attraction to making continuities with dramatic ideas rather than going a long way down an emotional journey . . . which didn't mean there wouldn't be very emotional things' (1997, p. 4). This quote illustrates the ways in which Joint Stock's perspective was influenced by Bertolt Brecht's theatrical innovations.

Brechtian influence

Since the Berliner Ensemble brought its production of Brecht's *Mother Courage* to London in 1956, Brecht's concepts have affected British theatre in diverse ways. Brecht's ideas have circulated so widely partially because he wrote groundbreaking theatre theory as well as dramatic works. Churchill acknowledges a general Brechtian influence in her work:

> I think for writers, directors and actors working in England in the seventies his ideas have been absorbed into the general pool of shared knowledge and attitudes, so that without constantly thinking of Brecht we nevertheless imagine things in a way we might not have without him.[20]

Stafford-Clark has referred to *Top Girls* as a 'domestic epic',[21] which illustrates a combination of the traditionally associated feminine realm with Brecht's epic theatre. Churchill's non-linear play structure and emphasis on ideas correspond to Brecht's concept of the epic theatre. Instead of following the realistic model of presenting a cohesive production, Brecht wanted the separate elements of the production to be obvious. In this way, the viewer does not become absorbed in the performance, but the 'spectator is given the chance to criticize human behavior from a social point of view' (1957, p. 86). By organizing the dramatic narrative in an episodic instead of linear fashion, Brecht intended the play's form to contribute to the audience's awareness. Brecht was very critical of the extreme emotionalism within Aristotelian-based theatre. By avoiding catharsis at the end of a production, Brecht hoped to motivate the audience to action. Churchill's refusal to provide her audience with clear answers or a closed, linear narrative is a way of achieving that goal.

In order to understand his influence on Churchill more fully, we need to examine some of the central terms that Brecht utilized to describe his epic theatre: alienation, gestus and historicization. Central to Brecht's theatre was the concept of Verfremdungsteffekt, which is commonly translated as alienation effect. Brecht used alienation effects in order to defamiliarize the audience with the existing societal order and attempt to come to a new understanding. In order to achieve such alienation, Brecht proposes an acting style where the actor avoids becoming transformed into his or her character, by frequently signalling to the audience that he or she is aware of the performance. To describe this concept, Brecht provides an example of a man on the street describing and acting out an accident to a passer-by. He advises that actors should follow the example of the man on the street, remaining self-aware and thinking of themselves in the third person, as though asking the spectator, 'Isn't it just like that?'[22] Brecht also commonly achieved alienation effects through the use of distancing scenic devices such as placards and slides.

Brecht's gestus is a gesture intended to demonstrate social, not just individual, relations. For example, from a Brechtian perspective, the way Gret eats her soup does not just say something about her as an individual, but shows her peasant class, the scarcity of food during wartime, and her economic relation to those around her. In 'Gestic feminist criticism', Elin Diamond argues that feminists can utilize Brechtian gestus as a useful tactic to alienate gender from the body in order to cause audience members to rethink their own gender identifications. Diamond argues that the portrayal of Pope Joan vomiting at the end of the first act is a gestus representing her female body's revulsion towards the misogyny of Western religion, of which she has been a figurehead (1997, p. 88). In *After Brecht: British Epic Theater*, Janelle Reinelt provides a further example of gestus, citing Angie's act of trying on the dress that Marlene gives her as revealing the gap between Angie's world and Marlene's world. When the dress is too small, history has become marked out on Angie's body (1996, pp. 91–2).

Brecht utilized historicization techniques in order to emphasize the possibility of political change, insisting on keeping past periods' 'impermanence always before our eyes, so that our own period can be seen to be impermanent too'.[23] Theatre-makers present historical incidents in order to proclaim that 'it could have been otherwise' and that our current time does not have to remain the same either (Reinelt, 1996, p. 10). The songs in *Vinegar Tom* provide examples of historicization, bringing past witch-hunts to bear on current societal scapegoating. Reinelt sees the sharp contrast between *Top Girls'* dinner scene and the contemporary scenes as utilizing historicizing techniques (2000, p. 179). Additionally, Churchill and Brecht's utilization of Brueghel's *Dulle Griet* can be seen as an exemplifying their shared investment in the working class. Churchill's understanding of the figure parallels with Brecht's description of Griet as 'helpless and handicapped, [with] the features of a servant . . . The Fury defending her pathetic household goods with the sword. The world at the end of its tether.' [24]

The clearest parallel between Churchill and Brecht is their commitment to Socialist politics. Following from Marx's critique of capitalism, Socialists believe in state-supported services, such as health, education and welfare systems.[25] The Labour party, which included some Socialist ideas, gained support from working-class communities through their support of unions. However, during the 1980s, Labour lacked the political power to challenge Thatcher's Conservative party. Socialist playwrights were more radical than their Labour counterparts, aiming to mobilize the public by portraying working-class communities, and highlighting the disparity between the rich and poor. Churchill insists that most art has political implications, but that works such as hers 'usually only gets noticed and called "political" if it's against the status quo',[26] echoing Brecht's argument that 'for art to be "unpolitical" means only to ally itself with the "ruling" group' (1957, p. 196). Critics single both playwrights' works out as political because they work to counter prevalent capitalist values, within the theatre world and society at large.

Style

Scholars have also referred to Churchill's style as postmodern.[27] Postmodernism can refer to multiple genres, including architecture, film, literature and studio art. Characteristics of postmodernity include the use of pastiche, fragmentation and irony. Pastiche means that the work refers to the styles of previous works or eras without evoking their historical weight. Therefore, postmodernism has an aesthetic characterized by surface instead of depth. Postmodernist works are considered fragmentary, resisting linear narratives and making contradictory, and often ironic combinations.[28]

Critics who see *Top Girls* as postmodern have tended to reference the dinner scene, with its fragmented dialogue and incongruous, often humorous juxtapositions. However, postmodernity has not often been associated with political movements, because it questions such fixed notions as truth and identity. While feminists who question the concept of gender may embrace postmodernist concepts, feminists who view gender identity as a unifying political category might see postmodernism as incompatible with their understanding of feminism,[29] and so resist considering such a feminist play to be postmodern.

As we have seen, *Top Girls* has strong political resonances in terms of its origins, influences and reception. Next, we will turn to exploring the political views conveyed in the play text itself.

Close reading of key scenes

This section engages in close readings of several important dramatic moments in *Top Girls*. As you will see, close readings are interpretive, and there can be multiple ways to understand a passage.

I examine a scene from each of the play's acts, paying attention to the scenes' themes, wording and subtext. I first explore the play's innovative opening act, highlighting the women's shared experience of losing children. Next, I look at the play's first employment interview, which broadens Churchill's critique of bourgeois feminism. Finally, I turn to the play's hard-hitting argument between Marlene and Joyce, in which Angie's maternity is revealed and which represents the culmination of the play's political drama.

Before turning to the passages, the play's title itself deserves close consideration. Churchill chose the title after contemplating calling the play *Heroines*, but deciding that the audience might not understand the irony of that title.[30] 'Top girls' initially seems to be complimentary, but the play is subsequently revealed to be critical towards 'top girls' such as Marlene and Margaret Thatcher. Marlene and all of the figures in the first scene can be considered the 'top girls' of their eras. They attempt to come together to celebrate a contemporary character's success. However, having established themselves as individual achievers, they find it difficult to celebrate as a community. To achieve 'top girl' status implies a singularity, and perhaps loneliness at the top. Furthermore, the play reveals Marlene to achieve 'top girl' status due not only to competing with other women, but also by taking advantage of her sister and by deserting her daughter. Churchill illustrates that there is only limited space at the 'top' of the career ladder, thereby critiquing the hierarchical capitalist economy. Additionally, by deciding to include 'girls' in the title, Churchill alludes to the patriarchal tendency to demean women as permanently juvenile. The 'clever girls' (58) at the dinner party and the 'tough bird[s]' (102) at the employment agency have evidently internalized such descriptions and so they have become part of their self-images.

In the first act, Pope Joan's story illustrates the play's themes of performed gender roles and lost infants. Joan's story also causes a shift in mood from celebration to the exploration of shared pain. Lady Nijo, who had her babies taken away from her, becomes interested in Joan's pregnancy and asks her to explain what happened to her baby. Marlene, perhaps alluding to her own past pregnancy, asks Joan if she considered getting rid of the baby. But Joan reflects that she had not talked to another woman since she was twelve and 'wasn't used to having a woman's body' (70). Joan's recollection of going into labour is particularly comical because she is so divorced from her woman's body and surprised by the process: she thought that the contractions must have been 'something I'd eaten' (71) and instead of spoiling the procession, she thinks she will 'just sit down for a minute'. Known for her intellect, she carries on until 'I couldn't plan things properly any more'. Used to an elevated status as Pope, she expresses shock at the animalistic status that her birthing pains lower her to: 'I heard sounds like a cow lowing, they came out my mouth . . . And the baby just slid out onto the road' (71).

The women unite in laughing at the resulting pandemonium and confusion of the church establishment, but the mood soon switches:

JOAN:	One of the cardinals said, 'The Antichrist!' and fell over in a faint.
	They all laugh
MARLENE:	So what did they do? They weren't best pleased.
JOAN:	They took me by the feet and dragged me out of town and stoned me to death.
	They stop laughing.
MARLENE:	Joan, how terrible.
JOAN:	I don't really remember.
NIJO:	And the child died too?
JOAN:	Oh yes, I think so, yes. (71)

When Joan recollects her stoning, the women feel the full force of the patriarchal establishment, reflected in the sudden silence. Marlene intends her comment 'They weren't best pleased' (71) to be an understatement, but she is not prepared for how much of an understatement it becomes. Although the revelation is startling, Churchill resists sentimentalizing Joan or her baby's death. Consistent with her emphasis on intellectual pursuits, Joan herself denies emotion and recalls only the bare facts of her murder. Although the infant's fate was likely to have been death, Churchill leaves open the tantalizing possibility that the child survived. As well as shifting the play's mood, Joan's recollection also calls attention to the scene's constructed nature. Although the characters comment on the extreme nature of Joan's death, they do not express surprise that she can remember her own death. While Marlene is evidently a contemporary character, the rest of the characters have apparently materialized for the dinner. The characters all accept their meeting as normal, having their acquaintance with Marlene in common.

Joan's story leads the other women to share their stories of lost children. Nijo recalls her four children who were taken from her, particularly her daughter who was adopted. By her fourth birth, Nijo reflects that even though her son was the more desired male infant, 'oddly enough I felt nothing for him' (72), which could be seen as a result of having had so many children previously taken from her. The only non-mother of the group is Isabella, and Churchill intersperses her descriptions of beloved horses with Nijo's recollections of her children. This combination can be interpreted as downplaying Nijo's losses, or to illustrate a contrast between their two stories.

The women's shared discussion of lost children notably affects Marlene's outlook. In contrast to Marlene's previous toast: 'We've all come a long way. To our courage and the way we changed our lives and our extraordinary achievements' (67), she now finds herself questioning, 'Oh God, why are we all so miserable?'(72).

However, Churchill quickly finds the humorous possibilities within even the direst of circumstances. Joan counters Marlene's question with the comical musing, 'The procession never went down that street again' (72), which succeeds in distracting Marlene from her gloominess. The women once again can make fun of the church establishment's need to reroute the papal procession and introduce a pierced chair to confirm the Pope's sex. The women laugh at the concept of a hole in the very seat of patriarchy, demeaning the concept of phallic power. They imagine conducting inspections, with Gret joining in enthusiastically and announcing, 'Balls!' and comparing 'Big one, small one' (73). The humour reaches a new level of bawdiness, temporarily diffusing the dark mood of introspection that Pope Joan's story inspired, and portraying female bonding.

Marlene's need to celebrate her accomplishments with imaginary women implies that she has no close friends to invite. The play's first act shows Marlene in a community of women from previous eras, but the play subsequently shows that she has minimal loyalty towards contemporary women. In Act Two, Churchill critiques the *Top Girls* Employment Agency where Marlene works as reinforcing gender oppression. Marlene's promotion loses its lustre when it becomes evident that she obtains her position of power by viewing all workers, male and female, as competition. This attitude partially explains why the employment agency does little to actually get the female workers careers that will advance them above the glass ceiling. Instead of presenting a means to unite women, the placements ultimately confirm the status quo. Marlene's interview with Jeanine exemplifies the interviewers' tactics. Churchill positions the scene as the opening to Act Two and the first contemporary scene at the employment agency. The scene is also Marlene's only interview and the first time that we see her work demeanour.

Marlene starts the interview by effectively putting Jeanine in her place. She is clearly not overly invested in Jeanine, being uncertain of her name. Marlene then lists Jeanine's qualifications; expressing her displeasure at her lack of an A-level or sufficiently high typing speeds. Although Jeanine reports that she is a secretary, Marlene initially doubts her, clarifying if she is actually a secretary of a lower-level typist. Jeanine describes her position as a secretary 'to three of them, really, they share me' (84), paralleling her position with being the collective property of her superiors. While Jeanine attempts to describe her co-workers' positions, such details are of little concern to Marlene and she cuts off the explanations.

Once she reveals her engagement, Marlene envisions Jeanine as a mother and subsequently assumes that Jeanine will not follow a significant career path. When Jeanine informs Marlene that she is saving to get married, Marlene immediately enquires: 'Does that mean you don't want a long-term job, Jeanine?' She advises Jeanine that it will help her job prospects if she does not inform employers that she is getting married and considers the fact that Jeanine does not wear a ring simply '[s]aves taking it off' (85). Jeanine's question, 'what if they ask?'(85), is left hanging in the air, with Marlene not considering it worthy of answering. The highest position that Marlene envisions for Jeanine in ten years is as a personal assistant, although to a higher-level executive. Jeanine does not seem inclined to plan ten years ahead, fearing 'I might not be alive in ten years'; but Marlene insists that she will be, assuming, 'You'll have children' (86).

Marlene makes certain that Jeanine has not consulted any competitive employment agencies, although she underplays this as not wanting to 'get crossed wires' (87). She warns Jeanine, 'If I send you that means I'm putting myself on the line for you' (87). When Jeanine hesitates regarding the position of a secretary to a marketing manager at a knitwear manufacturer, Marlene's next offer is more pedestrian, working as a secretary and receptionist at a lampshade company. Jeanine enters the interview hoping for a raise, a position in advertising, and the opportunity to travel. Instead, she gets an offer of the same paycheck at a lampshade company, and the potential to have power over other secretaries. Marlene points the last characteristic out to Jeanine, illustrating Marlene's priorities to be a 'top girl'. Marlene is so slickly convincing that Jeanine leaves with the intention of trying to prove herself to Marlene and her future employers.

An older woman, Louise, who is interviewed later in the play, assumes that it is the interviewer's 'job to understand me, surely. You asked the questions' (107). Louise has pointedly misunderstood the interviewer's intent, which is to categorize and expedite the process, and often to avoid understanding. Ostensibly assisting the women applicants, the agency takes few risks, opting to narrowly define what low-level jobs suit the women's skills. Therefore, *Top Girls* Employment Agency makes the glass ceiling all the more mysterious, because the women who claim to be deconstructing it actually reinforce the oppressive structure.

In order to climb as far as she can on the corporate ladder, Marlene disguises her own working-class background and personal history. In Act Three, Churchill reveals that Marlene's economic success is not only caused by her ambition, but is dependent on her sister's domestic labour. Churchill sets the scene up as a family celebration around the kitchen table, an intimate setting that becomes the site of a contentious debate. Marlene and Joyce are awkward towards each other from the opening, and their bitter disagreements illustrate how far apart the sisters have grown. The mounting differences between their politics are reflected by their perspectives on work and family, as well as their versions of a shared past and outlooks on the future.

The sisters' opposing views on family commitments initiate their heated argument. After Angie retires to bed, Marlene and Joyce's conversation quickly turns to another family member. Marlene sums up their mother's life as a 'Fucking waste', to which Joyce responds, 'Don't tell me' (132). Here, Joyce has abbreviated the expression 'you don't need to tell me', implying that she already knows what Marlene is saying. But her repeated rebuttal of 'Don't talk to me' reveals Joyce's driving force behind her lines: an effort to silence Marlene's voice. Joyce then repeatedly insists 'we can do without you' (132), with 'we' referring to herself, her mother and Angie. Here, Joyce establishes a binary division between the community that she identifies with and Marlene, who has excluded herself from that unity. Because Joyce dutifully visits her mother every week, she feels well aware of her mother's struggles. Joyce insists that 'Somebody has to', being bound as a caretaker and member of a larger working-class community. Marlene attempts to escape such moral entanglements by claiming: 'No they don't / Why do they?' (133). Here, Marlene expresses her worldview in its essence, proposing a new world order of individualism, and thereby challenging the traditional obligations towards familial and societal ties.

Marlene insists that she had to escape the life that she had envisioned in her future – that of entering into a working-class marriage and subsequently becoming subordinate to her husband's demands. She envisions the scenario and the torrent of verbal abuse: 'Don't you fucking this fucking that fucking bitch . . . fucking tell me what to fucking do fucking'(133). Marlene has used so many expletives that the sentence structure has been repeatedly disrupted and rendered almost superfluous. Joyce interjects a more mild 'Christ' to attempt to get Marlene to stop her rambling imitation of working-class chauvinism. Then Joyce succeeds in getting Marlene's attention by divulging the underlying issue between the two sisters: 'I don't know how you could leave your own child' (133). Joyce's comment is a revelation to the audience, who until that moment was led to believe that Angie was Joyce's daughter. Marlene may have been anticipating Joyce's sentiments however, as illustrated by her prompt response: 'You were quick enough to take her.' Marlene elaborates, 'You couldn't have one so you took mine' (133), pointedly avoiding using the word baby and portraying Angie in market terms, as an object of exchange. Although Marlene keeps quiet about her 'lost child' in the first act, the revelation of Angie's true parentage connects Marlene's past with the stories articulated by the women at the dinner party.

When Joyce implies that Marlene would not be making the same salary now if she had raised Angie, Marlene paints a picture of a career woman with it all: 'I know a managing director who's got two children, she breast feeds in the boardroom, she pays a hundred pounds a week on domestic help alone and she can afford that because she's an extremely high-powered lady earning a great deal of money' (134). The superwoman figure sounds more like a media creation than a career woman that Marlene might actually know, which is supported by the fact that Marlene avoids referring to this acquaintance by name. Additionally, Churchill has previously portrayed all of Marlene's co-workers as single women, and Marlene advised Jeanine to avoid letting employers know that she was engaged or contemplating having children. The image of Marlene's acquaintance breastfeeding in the boardroom seems especially incongruous considering the fast-paced, aggressive and male-emulating work environment that Churchill portrayed in the previous act. Moreover, Joyce exposes Marlene's idealized portrayal as irrelevant: 'So what's that got to do with you at the age of seventeen?' (134). Marlene's ability to join the workforce is dependent on the exploitation of Joyce's uncompensated labour in the domestic sphere.

Joyce debunks Marlene's 'clever girl' image: 'for someone so clever you was the most stupid, get yourself pregnant, not go to the doctor, not tell' (134). Churchill has Joyce use improper grammar while insulting another character's intelligence, which would typically undermine Joyce's point. Joyce places responsibility on Marlene, describing her as getting herself pregnant while never mentioning the father. However, Joyce's point remains poignant because it significantly undermines Marlene's public persona. Marlene has insisted that Joyce is jealous of her clever status, and describes cleverness as the shared characteristic between her and the women in the first act. Joyce's recollection reveals Marlene, who portrays herself as the ultimate 'go-getter', as nonetheless paralysed by inaction when she became pregnant at 17. Perhaps like Pope Joan, Marlene disassociated herself from her female body, denying her pregnancy as long as possible and thereby limiting her options. Marlene continues to 'not tell', maintaining the secret of her motherhood even during the first act when the women commiserate regarding their struggles surrounding childbirth and lost children.

Both characters remember their pivotal discussion in which Joyce came to assume responsibility for Angie, but Churchill leaves the factors that went into Joyce and Marlene's decision-making provocatively vague. Marlene recalls: 'You said I'm glad you never got rid of it, I'll look after it, you said that down by the river. So what are you saying, sunshine, you don't want her?' (134). Marlene repeatedly refers to the baby as 'it', minimizing her biological connection to Angie, and then shifts to using the pronoun 'her' when referring to Angie in the present tense, individualizing Angie to maximize Joyce's guilt. That their initial discussion would have occurred outside of the house and out of parental earshot makes logical sense. Churchill specifies that their conversation occurred 'down by the river', evoking a comforting image of nature and sisterly togetherness. However, Marlene subverts such comforting connotations by sarcastically referring to Joyce as 'sunshine'. Although the sisters made their choices while surrounded by a natural environment, the ramifications have led to a sisterhood distanced from natural bonds.

Joyce tells Marlene to listen to her while she recalls a painful memory, which serves as a main source of her animosity towards Angie and Marlene:

JOYCE: Listen when Angie was six months I did get pregnant
            and I lost it because I was so tired looking after your
            fucking baby/ because she cried so much – yes I did
            tell
MARLENE: You never told me.
JOYCE: you – / and the doctor said if I'd sat down all day
            with
MARLENE: Well I forgot.
JOYCE: my feet up I'd've kept it. (135)

Marlene's listening abilities are evidently dependent upon her will to comprehend. She admits that she forgot about Joyce's miscarriage, or has denied that it was partially due to Joyce's caring for her own biological daughter. She continues her avoidance of the subject, first by interrupting Joyce with the admission that she has had two abortions, and then dismissing the subject of babies as 'boring', 'messy' and, in their most removed and clinical form, as 'gynaecology' (135).

Despite her resentment, Joyce still views Angie as her child and she expresses her major fear: 'stop trying to get Angie off of me' (135). Marlene had made a halfhearted offer to assume responsibility for Angie: 'I'll take her, / wake her up and pack now' (134). While this may express a passing fancy or a threat to Joyce, Marlene is clearly too self-involved to actually care for the troubled Angie. While Joyce responds to Marlene's literal offer to take Angie, her fear can also refer to the symbolic allure that Marlene represents to Angie. Indeed, Marlene's high-paced, glamorous lifestyle does eventually induce Angie to leave Joyce and their bleak surroundings. As much as they resent each other for personal reasons, when Marlene starts to cry, Joyce makes conciliatory efforts and the women are able to resume a calmer discourse.

However, the sisters are unable to bridge the widening political gap between them. Once she distances herself from identifying with her family's working-class status, Marlene has a bright outlook for the future:

MARLENE: I think the eighties are going to be stupendous.
JOYCE: Who for?
MARLENE: For me./ I think I'm going up up up.
JOYCE: Oh for you. Yes, I'm sure they will. (137)

Marlene emphasizes her enthusiasm for the future by her use of repetition, in which she envisions herself steadily ascending the career ladder. However, to Joyce, Marlene's prioritizing of 'me' is the most telling. Marlene may be correct in seeing herself as being able to prosper, but Joyce points out that this affluence comes at the expense of the majority. The sisters' debate takes on an increasingly heated tone once Marlene voices her support for Margaret Thatcher's Conservative government. Joyce challenges Marlene's praise of Thatcher as the first woman prime minister, instead portraying Thatcher as a fascist: 'What good's first woman if it's her? I suppose you'd have liked Hitler if he was a woman. Ms Hitler. Got a lot done, Hitlerina' (138). Joyce's use of hyperbole illustrates her rising emotionality. However, Marlene values Thatcher as a role model of a 'tough lady', parallelling Thatcher with the 'tough birds' at the employment agency. Likewise, she echoes the fast-paced office dialogue with a list of superlatives for Thatcher: 'Terrifico. Aces. Right on' (138). Marlene attempts to get the last word in the argument, when she goads Joyce: 'Not a word about the slimy unions will pass my lips' (138). Marlene knows that Joyce supports the unions, following their father's political stance.

Marlene views her mother as a victim of her father's alcohol-fuelled domestic violence, while Joyce perceives both her parents as having been oppressed by the upper classes. Joyce explains why Angie will not make it in terms of class:

JOYCE: Because nothing's changed and it won't with them in.
MARLENE: Them, them./Us and them?
JOYCE: And you're one of them. (140)

Joyce represents the world as being broken down into a clear dichotomy between 'us' and 'them'. 'Us' represents the working class since Joyce is a member of this group, working multiple cleaning jobs. 'Them' represents the group of economic oppressors, which Marlene joined once she gave up responsibility for her daughter and viewed life as a capitalist venture. Both characters acknowledge Joyce has 'what it takes' (141) to make it in the capitalist hierarchy, except perhaps the will to support the system. Marlene insists that the working class 'doesn't exist any more, it means lazy and stupid', with those who do not succeed economically simply lacking initiative. Marlene then unintentionally implies that class distinctions still exist, and that she has distanced herself from the class into which she was born, admitting, 'I don't like the way they talk' (139). Here, Marlene uses the 'us' versus 'them' terminology that she challenged previously. Marlene would have grown up speaking in a working-class vernacular, but she has consciously altered her speaking patterns to increase her chances of upward mobility.

Although Churchill depicts Joyce as a deeply flawed character and not as a political crusader, Churchill still gives her the upper hand in the debate with Marlene. Although Joyce does not seem to be able to channel her anger towards change, she directs her frustration towards symbols of power. Joyce recalls with pleasure, 'I spit when I see a Rolls Royce, scratch it with my ring' (139). Joyce confuses the Rolls Royce with a Mercedes and then corrects herself. The details are important to her memory of the event, which she admits was a one-time act of defiance. In her socioeconomic position, desecrating such symbols may be the closest that she can get to affecting the system that she resents. In contrast to the euphoric future that Marlene envisions, Joyce sees the 1980s as a time of class uprising. Joyce advises Marlene that the neighbours with whom Marlene had grown up would see her as an outsider and implicated in their oppression: 'So don't be round here when it happens because if someone's kicking you I'll just laugh' (140). Joyce's threat concludes the aggressive portion of the sisters' argument. After a silence, Marlene attempts to concede some of her statements by insisting that she doesn't 'mean anything personal'. However, the argument has become both personal and political, and for Joyce there is no retreating. Before exiting, Joyce tells Marlene that she does not think that the two sisters can consider each other to be friends, and rejects Marlene's attempt at a reconciliation: 'No pet. Sorry' (141). Churchill depicts Joyce as adhering to her political convictions while leaving Marlene with a drink and in a state of denial about her lack of a community.

Instead of providing a clear moral lesson, Churchill's play ends ominously. Angie enters in a half-awake state, apparently looking for her mother for comfort. In her night wanderings, Angie has found her biological mother, but Marlene denies the association:

ANGIE: Mum?
MARLENE: No, she's gone to bed. It's Aunty Marlene.
ANGIE: Frightening.
MARLENE: Did you have a bad dream? What happened in it?
           Well you're awake now, aren't you pet?
ANGIE: Frightening. (141)

Marlene assumes that Angie has simply had a bad dream, and tries to establish a difference between Angie's nightmare and reality. She addresses Angie as 'pet', the same colloquial term of endearment that Joyce has just used towards her. However, Angie repeats herself: 'Frightening,' implying that the real world that she faces is at least as disturbing as any nightmare. Churchill gives Angie the final word in the play, causing the audience to think about how the next generation will be affected by the political conflict expressed in the sisters' debate. 'Frightening' describes Angie's personal fear, and the antagonism between the sisters, but can also represent a bleak political outlook for the future.

Top Girls' time-shifting serves to increase the dramatic impact of the final debate scene. The play presents a time gap in order to give the audience perspective from which to view social change. Initially, Marlene refuses to acknowledge that Angie will not succeed in the job market even though she is enrolled in remedial classes and displays little ambition:

JOYCE: She's stupid, lazy and frightened, so what about her?

MARLENE: You run her down too much. She'll be all right.

JOYCE: I don't expect so, no. I expect her children will say
            what a wasted life she had. (140)

Joyce takes Marlene's description of the working class and applies it
to Angie, adding the significant term 'frightened' to describe her.
Having raised Angie, Joyce is well aware of how frightened the girl
feels even without being privy to Angie's night walking. Joyce
infers that Angie will further the cycle of class and patriarchal
oppression. When visiting with Angie and Joyce, Marlene asked
Angie if she would like to work with children, perhaps overly opti-
mistically seeing Angie as having the potential to be nurturing
(126). Marlene makes an accurate point when she observes that
Joyce insults Angie too much, but her assurance that Angie will 'be
all right' is revealed to be glibly optimistic.

A year later, Marlene agrees with Joyce's estimation: something
occurs in a year of puberty that nullifies any possibility for Angie.
When Angie arrives at the agency, Marlene does not initially recognize her, apparently misidentifying her as another anonymous
interviewee. Ultimately, Marlene assesses her daughter in a
detached manner, as she would one of her clients. Observing Angie
while she naps, Marlene quickly sums up her lack of potential,
seeing her as likely to work at a grocery store: 'Packer in Tesco more
like. She's a bit thick. She's a bit funny . . . She's not going to make
it' (120). Although presented as the end of the second act, this
would be the play's final line if the narrative is reordered chronologically. While Churchill leaves Angie and Marlene's relationship
unresolved, we expect that Marlene will refuse to provide Angie
with opportunities that might help her confidence, such as an
internship, education, or a nurturing family life. Thus, the audience
leaves the play trying to envision ways they might contribute to a
less 'frightening' future, where circumstances become more

hospitable to the next generation. Young women such as Angie may find themselves confused, but nonetheless continue searching for a middle way between Joyce's trapped resentment and Marlene's ruthless ambition.

Changing views of *Top Girls'* themes and theory

Top Girls' continued relevance is evidenced by the scope of discussion and inquiry that it has initiated. The play's subject matter has inspired controversies concerning women in the workplace and the role of motherhood. Partially due to the play's open-endedness and non-linearity, it has been the subject of many – often contradictory – interpretations. Therefore, this section examines the interpretations of Churchill's subject matter and stylistic innovations, paying special attention to Churchill's overlapping dialogue. Here, the emphasis is on scholarly reactions towards the play: the performance history chapter (Chapter 3) provides more information on newspaper reviewers' responses.

Since *Top Girls'* premiere, scholars' reception of the play has gone through multiple manifestations. Feminist theatre scholar Elaine Aston looks back on her view of *Top Girls* and reflects that her understanding of the play, along with her colleagues' views, shifted from a focus on the imaginative dinner scene to the politics of the kitchen scene, and now on to Angie's story (2003, p. 26). This section will build on Aston's insight, examining responses to the linguistic innovations of the first act, then to the socialist feminist ramifications of the kitchen debate between Joyce and Marlene, and concluding by examining the shift in reception towards Angie's story as a way to look towards the future.

Act One: overlapping dialogue
Since the play's premiere, audiences and critics have seen Churchill's overlapping dialogue technique as an innovation in

dramatic style. Many critics have applauded the act's surrealistic realm, which the medium of the theatre makes possible. However, critics have engaged in an ongoing debate concerning whether the first act's characters primarily challenge patriarchal values or perpetuate them. While a minority of critics have interpreted the first act as expressing the universal experience of women across history, many critics have pointed out that the women have all either assumed male roles or embody archetypical feminine qualities. Some critics argue that the women have internalized patriarchal standards in order to achieve success, and that they have a competitive attitude towards each other. Therefore, the characters remain limited by patriarchal expectations and cannot listen to each other's parallel struggles as women. In 'The father and the invisible patriarchy', Paul Rosefeldt takes the argument regarding patriarchy one step further and argues that the women are united by their relationships with their father, and are all either trying to follow their father's wishes or replicating their absent father (1995, p. 129). However, Rosefeldt's rather deterministic focus on the literal patriarch tends to downplay the characters' rebellious elements.

Critics have made different interpretations of the mood that the overlapping dialogue sets for the scene. Critical reception initially focused on the ways in which the overlapping dialogue illustrated that the women were not listening to each other. In 'The silencing of women in feminist British drama', Margarete Rubik argues that Churchill does not provide an 'authentic female voice' (1996, p. 177); and in *Retreats from Realism in Recent English Drama*, Ruby Cohn describes the women as 'selfishly alone' (1991, p. 132). The majority of critics portray the characters as egoists focusing on their own narratives.[31] Recently however, theorists have attempted to use linguistic analysis to rehabilitate the dinner guests and their methods of communication. In 'Deviant speech', Melody Schneider (2004) avoids depicting 'women's speech' as pre-determined, rather arguing that societal gender roles influence speech patterns.

Schneider perceives that as a group it is common for women to communicate collaboratively: to make comments, to complete another person's sentences, or to rephrase another's words. She sees the women in the first act as active listeners, expressing empathy. As proof, she points out that the characters do not seem to be widely insulted by the interruptions, and have heard each other (because they answer each other's questions). Schneider concedes that even if at times some of the characters are self-centred, their revelations build to a therapeutic release. Instead of being chaotic, she argues that the audience understands the main points of the characters' narratives, creating a continuously linked narrative. Additionally, she makes a valid argument that the office interview scenes, where subordinate characters are verbally cut off less frequently, are where they are more lastingly silenced.

The issue of how to interpret the silences in the scene has been equally contentious. Socialist feminist analysis has brought focus to the less vocal women at the dinner party. Amelia Howe Kritzer convincingly argues that the quantity of lines spoken by the characters correlates to their class status (1991, p. 144). Linda Fitzsimmons (1987, p. 20) sees Gret as important not just because she is the only working-class woman represented, but because she is the only character at the dinner to call for women's collective, as opposed to individual, resistance of oppression. Fitzsimmons points out that Churchill's changes in the dialogue from the script used in the original production to the published play call attention to Gret's message. Crucially, Churchill includes a personal motivation for Gret's political fight by adding that the soldiers had killed her children. Gret's speech originally had no interruptions, and that these were inserted emphasize the speech's importance, with the women telling each other to listen and emphasizing that Gret is leading a woman's fight. In contrast, Rubik argues that Gret and the women's violence would only establish another oppressive hierarchy (1996, p. 181).

Further debate ensued as to whether the restaurant setting trivializes the women's stories (Merrill 1988, p. 83). Dull Gret's stage actions accompany her silence through the majority of the scene, often resulting in her comic 'stealing' of the scene. The women narrate some very personal moments, and then turn to order their food. As Fitzsimmons (1987, p. 20) notes, in the final published version of the script Churchill adds that Nijo is laughing as well as crying at the end of the scene. Although some critics took the contradiction of emotions in the scene to be belittling, Fitzsimmons takes this final combination of joy and sorrow as leaving a possibility for hope. However, while some of the initial analysis overly stressed the women's antagonism and competitiveness, the pendulum may have swung too far to the other extreme here, with Schneider overstating the women's humanistic and charitable characteristics.

The waitress's silence has also been widely interpreted as illustrating Marlene and her guests' lack of consideration towards their working-class 'sister'. Here, Schneider seems to overstate her rehabilitation of the guests' attitudes, when she claims that she is neither surprised nor overly perturbed by the waitress's silence. While Marlene may speak more because she is the hostess, her ability to be the hostess and the women's treatment of the waitress still has deep class resonances. By performing everyday work onstage, the waitress is also able to draw the audience's attention and foreshadows the kitchen debate scene. By transitioning the play from the dinner party to the kitchen, Churchill exposes the working world that makes such extravagances possible.[32]

The kitchen debate: socialist feminist response
Overall, *Top Girls* has been understood along the lines of socialist feminism, with scholars such as Aston, Reinelt, Diamond and Fitzsimmons highlighting the work's critiques of Marlene as a representation of an extreme individualistic attitude that bourgeois feminism can foster. However, critical reception of the play has

sometimes overlooked Churchill's differentiation between types of feminisms. For instance, even the socialist feminist Michelene Wandor initially accused the play of glorifying bourgeois feminism, and criticized Churchill for not providing a clear feminist role model (1981, p. 173). More common has been the tendency to see the play as critical of feminism as a whole. For instance, in her article 'Caryl Churchill's *Top Girls* and Timberlake Wertenbaker's *Our Country's Good*', Christiane Bimberg interprets the play as encouraging a 'rethinking of the extreme consequences of hard-line feminist positions, a questioning of the propriety of adopting male modes of behaviour by working women' (1997, p. 405). Bimberg implies that the working woman was a step backwards for the feminists, leading to a need to 'soften' or feminize their positions. Likewise, in '"The personal is political" in Caryl Churchill's *Top Girls*: a parable for the feminist movement in Thatcher's Britain', Chantal Cornut-Gentille D'Arcy sees the play's main question as being: 'does contemporary feminism advocate living disguised as a man, forsaking one's origins and family, obeying absolutely the dictates of patriarchy?' (1995, p. 115). In this case, an analysis of women assuming roles that have been defined by patriarchy has resulted in an interpretation that seems to deflate contemporary feminism. Considering that such questions have even sprung from feminists' interpretations of the play, one can see that it is just a step further to interpreting the play as simply anti-feminist. However, such an interpretation works counter to both Churchill's intent in writing the play and to the political background that motivated her artistic statement.

In an interpretation which challenges the play's feminist effectiveness, in *Race, Sex and Gender in Contemporary Women's Theatre* (1999) Mary Brewer warns that Churchill's portrayal of Marlene could play into the contemporary backlash against feminism. Brewer contends that Churchill achieves a precarious balance between feminism and socialism in the play, which expects a lot of its audience. and argues that while the Brechtian techniques that Churchill employs may emphasize that motherhood is a constructed role and guard against Marlene being simplified as 'a bad mother' (1999, p. 75), Marlene's actions could imply to some that women should not engage in the public sphere and should return to a more traditionally domestic realm. However, Brewer implies that this is the risk that Churchill takes by her stylistic innovations (1999, p. 80). Indeed, Churchill has articulated that she does not want to spell out her political messages to her audience: and expecting less of one's audience does not seem a productive way forward for playwriting.

Critics who have villainized Marlene as an unfit mother have been countered by those who perceive the play's depiction of motherhood as being jointly affected by the capitalist and patriarchal systems. For instance, in her article 'Perceiving and performing Caryl Churchill: the drama of gender construction' (1999), Annette Pankratz refutes the simplistic interpretation that if Marlene would just transform into an attentive, domestic mother, the play's dilemma would be solved. Pankratz claims that many of the play's original critics measured Marlene by what they considered should have been her 'essential' or naturally determined inclination towards motherhood. Following such logic, Joyce and Angie's lack of a biological mother–daughter bond primarily caused their troubled relationship. Such interpretations could function to let Thatcher's economic policies off the hook and minimize Churchill's subversive tendencies. However, Pankratz argues that Churchill in fact portrays her characters in a stalemate in order to show the rigidness and social construction of gender roles, and to illustrate that one should not assume the 'naturalness' of the motherhood role. Although Joyce may have taken responsibility for raising Angie, Churchill resists depicting her as a 'good mother' alternative to Marlene. Joyce blames taking care of Angie for her miscarriage and often demeans Angie. The sisters are locked in a stalemate, resulting in a no-win situation for Angie, who represents the source of their conflict.

Angie's story

Instead of becoming a period piece, *Top Girls* has remained surprisingly current, with critics and audience members placing a new emphasis on Angie's story. Aston locates a trend in Churchill's work of portraying children at risk as widespread in a society that increasingly emphasizes capitalist individualism (2003, p. 23). While Helene Keyssar's initial account interpreted Marlene and Joyce's argument about Angie as being resolved (1984, p. 98), subsequent analysis has seen their conflict as provocatively left unsettled. Commentators have referred to the upcoming generation as 'Thatcher's Children', implying that the materialism of the 1980s had come to fruition in the 1990s, with the majority facing economic difficulties without adequate social programmes to assist them.[33] Therefore, critics have reinterpreted Angie's narrative as prophetically speaking for the generation of 'Thatcher's Children' who face an increasingly ambivalent future.

Angie's final word, 'Frightening', has left the play particularly open to interpretation, inspiring a wide range of views. The source of Angie's fears can be seen as her individual psyche: her nightmares, the antagonisms between her aunt and mother, and her desertion by her biological mother. In an attempt to find a literal reason for Angie's fear, Lizbeth Goodman questions whether Angie could have overheard Marlene and Joyce's argument and that is why she thinks that she is Marlene's daughter and is so 'frightened' at the end of the play. Churchill says that she intended Angie not to have heard the argument and that she meant Angie's belief that Marlene is her mother as an instance of wish fulfillment.[34]

However, Churchill leaves open the possibility that Angie could have overheard; considering the scene realistically, Angie's room would be nearby and the women's voices might have risen during their argument. In *Staging Motherhood* (2006), Jozefina Komporaly explores the ways in which Angie feels pulled towards her mother in the final scene and repeatedly claims Marlene as her mother. By rejecting Angie's hopes, Marlene re-enacts her initial desertion of Angie.

Rather than stemming from a purely psychological source, recent analysis has favoured seeing the play's final words as indicative of widespread societal ramifications of Thatcher's policies and the weakening of feminist influences. *Top Girls'* relationship to feminism has remained of key importance, although societal views of feminism have changed drastically since the play's premiere. In 1988, Janet Brown wrote that 'Caryl Churchill's *Top Girls* catches the next wave', predicting that the play expressed the next wave of feminism, which would not focus on individualism, but radically transform society (p. 117). However, such a radical transformation failed to materialize and currently people speak more about 'post-feminism'[35] than they do about such a 'third wave'. In *Overloaded: Popular Culture and the Future of Feminism* (2000), Imelda Whelehan locates a recent backlash against feminism within British pop culture. She argues that second-wave feminism is now dismissed on contradictory grounds, either as prudishly ineffectual or as leading to a usurpation of male power. While newspaper articles (such as the *Guardian's* 'Brave new age dawns for single women' (Hartley-Vrewer 1999)) predicted improving opportunities for single women in the new millennium, gains for women in the workforce were depicted as coming at the expense of men.[36] The backlash has fostered a return to more traditional gender expectations, which Whelehan terms 'retro-sexism' (2000, p. 11).

The playwriting world has reflected this state of affairs: while Churchill's work continues to flourish, women still face ongoing struggles for equal representation.[37] Although there are notable exceptions, *Top Girls* has not resulted in widespread emulation of the all-woman play,[38] leading the playwright Mark Ravenhill to query why the all-women production of *Top Girls* has not been as widely emulated as the all-male plays of David Mamet.[39] The comparative disparity may well reflect a move away from separatist feminist movements as well as the closure of many of the 1970s women theatre collectives during Thatcherism.

In a particularly retroactive move, women claiming feminist intentions have recently reclaimed the historical figure of Margaret Thatcher. During the mid-1990s, the Spice Girls declared Margaret Thatcher 'the original Spice Girl' (Whelehan 2000, p. 54); and in *New Feminism*, Natasha Walter has made efforts to rehabilitate Thatcher's image, highlighting her normalization of female success and transgression of class and gender barriers.[40] *Top Girls* can serve as a reminder of the political divisiveness manifested by Thatcherite policies that continue to affect Britain today. Looking back on the play, Jane de Gay argues that the play's structure foreshadows Thatcher's decline. De Gay (1998) argues that by portraying Marlene at the end of the play with her working-class background revealed and before she receives her promotion, Churchill effectively demotes Marlene. Viewed in light of Thatcher's fall from political grace, the play emphasizes that the patriarchal system does not offer even clever women such as Marlene or Margaret Thatcher a reliable way up the corporate or political ladder. Of course, such analysis has the benefit of hindsight, and it would be impossible for the play's original viewers to make such predictions.

Although the play's final moments are sobering, many critics have viewed *Top Girls'* radically non-linear fashion and multiple-role casting as emphasizing the potential for social change. Christopher Innes points out that 'the structure of the play offers a model of alternative ways of thinking' (2002, p. 517): each act does not lead to the next in a logical fashion, suggesting disruption and intervention. Ruby Cohn emphasizes that the play starts in a dream and ends in a nightmare (1991, p. 131). Extending the connection, Innes points out the intersection between Angie's 'frightening' and the last words of the Pope Joan's Latin speech 'terrorem'.[41] There-fore, the play can be seen as coming full circle while also having an open-ended conclusion, which is designed to promote social action. Furthermore, Keyssar emphasizes the political possibilities enabled by double casting, pointing out that theatrical transforma-tions remind the audience 'that our awe of the actor derives at least in part from the confirmation that *we* can become other, that *we* can change' (1984, p. 90). According to Keyssar, Marlene's inabil-ity to transform indicates not only her central status, but reflects the limited social ramifications of her goals (1984, pp. 97–8).

Typically, the portrayal of the next generation symbolizes the play's outlook on potential for the future, and critics remain divided regarding Angie and Kit's relationship. Paralleling the interpretation of Gret as a revolutionary figure of female solidarity, some critics have seen their friendship as providing an example of feminist loyalty. However, others see the relationship mirroring Joyce and Marlene's conflict, predicting that Kit's ambitions will lead her to desert Angie. The differing opinions towards the girls' friendship are encapsulated in contrasting views towards their friendship rites. Rubik provocatively sees Angie's sucking of Kit's bloody finger as a 'grotesque inversion' of Germaine Greer's influ-ential *The Female Eunuch*, in which Greer writes: 'If you think you are emancipated, you might consider the idea of tasting your men-strual blood – if it makes you sick, you've a long way to go, baby' (Rubik 1996, p. 179 n. 2). Rubik implies that because Angie included Kit in an act, which Greer characterized as solitary, the girls invert Greer's concept of emancipation. In contrast, Kom-poraly views Angie and Kit's sharing of the taboo-breaking ritual as defining Angie to be the 'only genuine feminist character in the play, having understood the importance of female community' (2006, p. 52).

In 'Secrets as Strategies for Protection and Oppression in *Top Girls*' (1998), Harry Lane provocatively parallels the girls' fort and rebelliousness with the Greenham Common Women's Peace Camp, which was set up in 1981 in protest against the housing of the American Cruise missiles. He reasons that Kit's fear of nuclear war and Angie's secret notebook to take over the world reflect Thatcher's increase in state security and censorship. He argues that the secrets and revelations that occur throughout the play highlight the Thatcherite infringements on civil liberties. Lane's interpretation widens the perspective on the play to include the divisions created by recent US and British military involvement. Such an interpretation calls for a feminism that coincides with Churchill's recent anti-war emphasis.

3 Production History

While the previous chapter viewed *Top Girls* as a written text, this one explores the play as a theatrical event. First, the chapter looks at the play's premiere production, and the ways in which Thatcher's political career influenced the reception of the play in Britain. It then compares and contrasts different American and European interpretations of the play, and highlights the ways in which the play's revivals reflect changing political climates. While the last chapter focused on scholarly response to the play text, this chapter utilizes excerpts from theatre critics' reviews in order to reconstruct the effects of the play in performance. Additionally, this chapter looks at a recent film version of the play, and the changes caused by this change in medium.

British productions

Stafford-Clark recalls his reaction to being asked if he was aware of the play's significance when he first read *Top Girls*: 'I received the script piecemeal and . . . it wasn't quite like that. Actually it's never like that . . . You're attempting to orchestrate chaos on a daily basis. "Triumph and disaster" hover like vultures over the whole journey.'[1] Although Stafford-Clark was familiar with Churchill's experimentation, the opening dinner scene was particularly challenging to stage. Churchill recalled that when writing the dinner scene she decided to break up each character's narrative thread: 'I first wrote a draft of the dinner scene with one speech after another and then realized it would be better if the talk overlapped.'[2]

Luckily, Stafford-Clark considered the author's presence as essential during the rehearsal process, and Churchill's contribution assisted in discovering the way to perform the first scene. The actress Lesley Manville recalled: 'Max did this very brave thing, which was admit that the first scene was a mystery to him, that he was having trouble seeing his way through it. We all were there and we all solved the problem. It was a minefield, that first scene.'[3] Although Churchill does not provide the name of the restaurant in the play text, from the first production onwards many productions have staged it at the aptly named Prima Donna Restaurant. The dinner scene turned out to be the one most noted by critics in the play's first run.

Top Girls premiered at the Royal Court Theatre on 28 August 1982, to mixed reviews. Although Stafford-Clark recorded in his journal that he thought *Top Girls* was the best play he had ever directed, he summed up how he perceived the reaction: 'First night. Peer-group approval. Critical disapproval.'[4] However, the critics were not as negative as Stafford-Clark perceived. For instance, Carol Rumens identified the play's two central conflicts as familiar dramatic territory during the 1980s: 'Patriarchy vs. Women' and 'Us vs. Them'. Although she describes the play as 'untidy', she recognized Churchill's originality in blending the two themes while making Joyce and Marlene both symbolic and credible characters.[5] When reviewed in the 1980s, Churchill found herself in a double bind, recalling: 'I'm accused of being both too optimistic and too pessimistic . . . and of being too philosophical and too aesthetic and not sufficiently political.'[6]

British understanding of the play hinged on the ups and downs of Thatcher's career, and her ongoing legacy. The play was initially staged before the full ramifications of Thatcher's economic policies had become apparent. Subsequent revivals led to Marlene's enthusiasm for the prime minister having additional significance. Wolfgang Huber, the dramaturg of the Austrian premiere, asked Churchill whether Marlene would still defend Thatcher's policies in 1986, to which Churchill replied: 'Unfortunately she does still have supporters here and I think Marlene might well be among them . . . I think what they say would still stand up in 1984, though a line like "I think the eighties are going to be stupendous" couldn't come much later than that.' By referring to the pivotal year 1984, Churchill is indirectly referring to the antagonism surrounding the Miners' Strike. However, Churchill perceives that the shift in perception that the strike created only adds to the scene's impact: 'Dramatically, considering the effects on the audience of hearing this support for Thatcher at the moment . . . I quite like the irony. I had never intended them to agree with Marlene's argument after all.'[7] The 1991 production occurred just after Thatcher's departure from office. Critics and audiences received it as a state of the nation play, looking at the divisions between 'us' and 'them' in the economic climate left after Thatcher's years in office.[8]

The play's recent productions have provided audiences with the opportunity to look back at the 1980s and consider the decade's influence. By Thea Sharrock's 2000 production at the Battersea Arts Centre, 'the line "I think the eighties are going to be stupendous" was greeted by a guffaw'.[9] Sharrock was the recipient of the James Menzies-Kitchen Award for young directors and chose to revive *Top Girls*, indicating the interest that the younger generation continues to have in the play. She resolved the challenge of how to stage the first act by devising a striking set piece, which captured the audience's attention. The dinner guests sat around a table, with the floor and table revolving slowly in order to provide the audience members with different perspectives of the characters. Subtle spotlights focused the audience's attention, creating a feeling of eavesdropping.[10] Working with Churchill's input, Sharrock adhered to the playwright's preference for three acts, although the original production included only one intermission after the first act. The three-act format splits the play into three distinct times and perspectives, with Churchill considering the middle act to be Angie's story.[11]

Although reviewers tend to agree that *Top Girls* remains timely, they differ in opinion as to what allure the play holds for each generation. In 2000, Lyn Gardner's interpretation of the play continued to follow materialist feminist concepts: 'Churchill points out that women's social progress cannot be separated from economic conditions . . . For every "top girl" there is a Dull Gret or Angie. It is they who become the army of underpaid, undervalued domestics who support the high fliers.' To Gardner the play represents not how far we've come, but the converse: 'In 1982, Marlene seemed a Thatcherite monster. Twenty years on she is all around us and we hardly notice. Frightening.'[12] In contrast, Benedict Nightingale took the 1991 revival as an opportunity to predict that the play's refusal to depict a triumphant feminist history would anger the doctrinaire feminists 'to be found policing Women's Studies in some modern universities' by portraying Marlene's misuse of the feminist inheritance from 'these excitedly chattering pioneers'.[13]

In 2000, Brian Logan suggests that the gender divisions depicted in the play are dated, proposing '*Top Boys* anyone?'[14] Logan implies that the play's conflict between parenting and career is no longer gender specific: contemporary fathers take more active roles in raising their children, and their concerns would be more interesting to address than career women's ongoing struggles over childcare. However, Logan does not take into account that male playwrights and male-focused plays have remained dominant since *Top Girls'* first production. All-women productions have become rarer, with women's theatre groups facing funding struggles. Therefore, plays examining male issues remain typical, while plays such as *Top Girls* provide much needed exceptions.

US productions

Stafford-Clark remembers the marketing trick that eventually paid off, establishing *Top Girls'* success on both sides of the Atlantic. Stafford-Clark took the Royal Court production of *Top Girls* to New York, billing the play as having been a hit in England, which resulted in a US success. When the play returned to the Royal Court in February 1983 it was billed as a New York hit, which favourably influenced reviewers and audience members: only then did *Top Girls* became a hit in Britain.[15]

Top Girls became the first of many of Churchill's plays to be produced at Joseph Papp's Public Theater as part of an exchange programme with the Royal Court Theatre. The off-Broadway run opened on 28 December 1982, and went on to win Obies for best play, director and ensemble cast. However, Stafford-Clark recalls that success brought complications for the production quality: when the play transferred to a bigger stage in New York, the audience members sat too far away, and the dinner scene's overlapping dialogue became indecipherable. He estimates that the conversation can only be properly heard within 400- to 500-seat theatres.[16]

Initially, critics found themselves especially confused by Marlene as the central character, unable to categorize her in a satisfactory manner. For instance, John Russell Taylor asked: 'Well is she a heroine or isn't she?'[17] Stylistically, critics have often been split on whether they appreciated the innovation of the first act or the realism of the second act more. For example, while admiring the 'tour de force' of the first act, Brad Rossenstein of *The San Francisco Bay Guardian* found 'disappointing elements of cliché' in the second and third acts.[18] While British critics may have recognized the elements of the state of the nation debate in the third act, Rossenstein critiques the characters as being psychologically underdeveloped.

Furthermore, Churchill's class critique sometimes did not translate to American critics. For instance, Frank Rich of *The New York Times* complained:

> The absence of the middle range – of women who achieve without imitating power-crazed men and denying their own humanity – is an artificial polemical contrivance that cuts the play off at its heart. We're never quite convinced that women's choices are as limited . . . Even in England, one assumes, not every woman must be either an iron maiden or a downtrodden serf.[19]

Rich sees the class disparity as reflecting specifically English stereotypes, and wants a positive representation of the middle ground. However, Churchill intended to avoid spelling out her play's political message, insisting that 'I quite deliberately left a hole in the play, rather than give people a model of what they could be like. I meant the thing that is absent to have a presence in the play.'[20] Churchill's decision encourages her audience members to engage actively with the production, envisioning what kind of character could represent the middle ground between Marlene and Joyce's viewpoints. Through this process, the play achieves a political goal, causing its audience members to consider the balance necessary between individual goals and community responsibility.

Since its New York premiere, *Top Girls* has continued to be staged frequently throughout the USA, implying the play's ongoing political relevance. The director of the *Top Girls* revival at the 2005 Williamstown Theater Festival, Jo Bonney, argues that the play's 1980s conflicts speak clearly to America's recent concerns:

> There are many similarities between Thatcher's England and America in 2005. In both cases, we see growing divisions between political parties, between liberals and conservatives, between the haves and the have-nots. In fact it's eerily familiar . . . the play is not just about feminism, it's not just about the political context – it's about an economic climate. If you have

money, you can do anything. Class dictates the choices available to women.[21]

Recent West Coast productions have included professional productions at ACT Theater, San Francisco's Exit Stage Left Theater, American Conservatory Theater, and college productions such as at the University of California, Irvine.

In 2003, Casy Stangl directed a notable production at the Guthrie Theater in Minneapolis. The dinner scene featured partially transparent screens depicting images of contemporary icons, which loomed over the long table where the historical women dined. For instance, Barbra Streisand contrasted with the image of Gret, providing an ironic distance. A portrait of Madonna, the Material Girl herself, decorates the workspace, with metal beams separating off different cubicle spaces. During the dinner scene, the historical figures remained frozen until Marlene enters and unfroze them. In a marked difference from the original stage directions, Stangl chose to mute the other dinner guests' dialogue, so that each speaker could be heard in turn.

The play has tended to be understood in terms of class conflict, but Stangl extends the play's relevance to include race relations. Stangl's most significant change occurred in choosing to cast the waitress as a black actress (Isabell Monk O'Connor). While the theatre scholar Dimple Godiwala imagines the significance of this,[22] the reviewer Alison Weir does not comment on the casting choice: she does not even list the waitress character, although she mentions that Monk O'Connor portrays Kit.[23] While the casting choice may not have appeared worthy of mention by all of the play's contemporary critics, the choice is especially relevant when looking at scholarly interpretations of the dinner scene. By deciding to portray the waitress as a black woman, Stangl has widened the implications of the other characters' silence towards her. While scholarly critics of the initial production focused on the class dynamics in these 'top girls' ignoring their working-class 'sister', in this production the dinner guests exclude a black woman's point of view in their discussion. Conversely, Stangl's choice to cast Monk O'Connor as Kit, a young woman who is more clever and more motivated than Angie, provides an element of hope in the production's racial politics.

European premieres

While Churchill works closely with the director on the first few productions of her works, after that she decides to let them go so directors can interpret the plays for themselves.[24] However, Churchill recalls two premieres that subverted the messages that she had written into *Top Girls:*

> In Greece where the working woman is rarer than in England, they saw the play as saying that women shouldn't go out to work – they took it to mean what they were wanting to say about women themselves, which is depressing . . . In Cologne, Germany, women characters were played as miserable and quarrelsome and competitive at the dinner . . . The waitress slunk about in a catsuit like a bunny girl and Win changed her clothes on stage in the office. It just turned into a complete travesty of what it was supposed to be.[25]

The German director's sexualized costume choices have no indications within the script to support them, and appear to reflect the misogynistic tendencies of mainstream theatre.

The Greek interpretation of the play as anti-career women is echoed in various critical receptions of the play, although perhaps in not as pronounced a way because working women are more common in Britain and the USA. For instance, Rossenstein sums up the play as 'a pointed critical look at the rarity of women in positions of power'.[26] While Churchill does illustrate the effects of the glass ceiling, more women in positions of power, as Marlene understands power, would not initiate the social change that the play calls for. In the *Independent*, Brian Logan claims that Churchill is asking: 'Must female emancipation . . . come at the expense of traditional femininity?'[27] While Churchill acknowledges that she conceived Marlene as adopting masculine characteristics in her career mindedness, Logan overstates the play's nostalgia for traditional feminine values. According to Logan's reading, the play's central conflict might as well be the difference between Marlene, the so-called 'emancipated' woman, and Mrs Kidd, the 'traditional' wife. Each of these reviews contains elements of the play's critique while ignoring others.

Film version

The filming of *Top Girls* occurred while a particularly significant transition was occurring in British politics: although it was produced between April and May 1991, while the Conservatives were still in power, it was distributed after Thatcher's surprise resignation on 22 November 1990.[28] The film was developed as a learning tool for schools, with an introduction and interviews at the end of the production. Due to Lizbeth Goodman's introductory analysis, the viewer already knows some background about the play, and has been instructed to pay attention to gender role-playing and who has the power to speak. Goodman also poses questions about the play's relevancy regarding both genders, and whether viewers consider it relevant today.

The major scriptural change that was made for the film version was the decision to move Jeanine's interview scene to the beginning of the film. Stafford-Clark proposed the change as a concession to a television audience's shorter attention span.[29] Although Churchill agreed with the decision, she noted that by filming Marlene's subsequent entry to the restaurant, the play got off to a slower start. By opening with Jeanine's interview, the film version starts on an ominous note, underscored by the foreboding music which underscores Marlene's intimidating demeanour. When Jeanine insists, 'I can't think about ten years,'(86) the subtitle 'The 1980s' immediately follows her words, emphasizing that it has been ten years since Churchill's play was written. Therefore, Churchill's original intent to have the audience believe that they are watching a celebratory piece, which then morphs into a critique, is altered. The first image of the film is Jeanine looking worried while waiting for Marlene's assessment. By seeing Marlene's brisk attitude towards her client, the audience already has a context from which to judge her subsequent hostess personality.

The film adaptation most obviously alters the effect of the dinner scene. The scene is set in a cavernous and sleek modern restaurant, with faux grey marble pillars. Marlene enters walking confidently down a curving stairwell, literally a 'top girl' looking down on the table. There is a water fountain behind the table, which Pope Joan plays in during the chaos at the end of the scene. Unlike in a theatrical performance, where the audience's eyes can wander to whichever character interests them, in the filmed dinner scene the choices are made for them, with the framing of the shot controlling their view. The sound of other competing voices also fades, so that portions of dialogue get emphasized instead of the full script. Gret's actions were given camera time, capturing her stealing bread and silverware, and scratching herself with a fork. As Gret slurped her soup, the camera also captured Isabella Bird's delicate manners next to her, causing the eye to compare the two characters. The waitress's presence is not as evident in the film version because the camera does not follow her much. The actress seems to mirror the emotions of the guests, joining in raising a toast of the brandy at the end of the scene.

It took three days to film the 40-minute dinner-party scene. The film crew shot from various angles, including close-ups and with cameras circling the outside of the table. They then used another table with a hole in the middle, so that the camera angle could give the viewer the impression that they were sitting at the table.[30] There were notable close-ups on Joan's face when she concluded that her baby had most probably died, and on Gret when she describes how the soldier ran a sword through her baby. The camera intervenes the most directly after Griselda's line, 'It was always easy because I always knew I would do what he said' (77) (referring to her giving her children away to Walter). The pause that Churchill designated in the script was particularly long, as the camera slowly panned around the table to each woman's discontented reaction until Isabella's droll line: 'I hope you didn't have any more children' (78).

In her examination of the film's costuming, Jane De Gay characterizes the historical women's life stories and attention to clothing as reminiscent of familiar 'Cinderella narratives', which reveal Marlene's and Thatcher's positions as 'top girls' to be precarious (1998, p. 112). De Gay also points out the political symbolism of the play's clothing, which is culturally specific. For instance, in the dinner scene in the film version, Marlene was dressed in a blue dress, which De Gay argues emphasizes her parallels with Margaret Thatcher and the Conservative party. In the final scene, Marlene sheds her blue jacket, revealing a red shirt – understood in Britain to represent class solidarity.[31] This connotation is opposite to typical US associations, where the Democrats are associated with blue and the Republicans with red. In contrast with the BBC film production, in the Guthrie production Marlene (Bianca Amato) wore red in the dinner scene and blue in the workplace, but without any of the socialist connotations that De Gay located in the British context.

The film's second and third acts are more realistic than the stage version, with Joyce's backyard and kitchen being particularly cluttered with everyday objects. However, some of Churchill's theatrical innovations differentiate the film from realism. While the first act's fantastical blending of time periods stands out, in the second act the cross-casting also calls attention to the fictional status of the film. Stafford-Clark and Churchill had discussed discarding the multiple-role casting choices, since the BBC budget would have allowed them to hire more actors.[32] Although they eventually decided to retain the multiple-role casting, the technique does not emphasize the film actors' versatility in the same way as it would onstage. While audience members of a theatre production are often amazed by the rapid way in which an actor can switch roles, in the back of their minds film viewers are savvy enough about filming processes to know that time can lapse between the scene changes and character transformations. On the other hand, the film's cross-casting still provocatively parallels historical and contemporary women's narratives. With the closer view available in film, the multiple-role casting is especially evident, particularly in the portrayals of girls by adult actresses. Furthermore, the film version builds upon the play's reputation, which has already been established as employing multiple-role casting techniques.

While _Top Girls'_ initial audiences viewed the play as a current political piece, subsequent revivals have resonated in ways that could not have been predicted by the play's initial audiences, or by Churchill herself. The ongoing interest in _Top Girls_ implies a continued interest in women's dilemmas, and a need to come to terms with the class and wealth disparity that still divide Britain. Although reviewers were initially unsure about the play, subsequent critics have recognized _Top Girls'_ influence and have treated the play as a contemporary classic. Few critics now question Churchill's political credentials, while her philosophical inclinations and attention to aesthetics have provided her work with lasting relevance.

Top Girls premieres

1982   The Royal Court Theatre, London (opening 28 August)
Max Stafford-Clark, Director
Peter Hartwell, Scenic Design
Selina Cadell, Pope Joan/Louise
Lindsay Duncan, Lady Nijo/Win
Deborah Findlay, Isabella Bird/Joyce/Mrs Kidd
Carole Hayman, Dull Gret/Angie
Lesley Manville, Patient Griselda/Nell/Jeanine
Gwen Taylor, Marlene
Lou Wakefield, Waitress/Kit/Shona[33]

Top Girls transferred to Joseph Papp's Public Theater in New York, presented by the New York Shakespeare Festival. The play ran at the Public Theater from 21 December 1982 until 29 May 1983. In March 1983 the British cast was replaced with a US cast.[34]

1983   Australia (Nimrod Theatre, Sydney); Sweden (Dramaten, Stockholm); Japan (Bungei-za Le Pilier, Tokyo); West Germany (Schauspielhaus, Cologne); Greece (National Theatre, Athens); Switzerland (Schauspielhaus, Zurich)

1984   Denmark (Aarhus Theatre); Norway (Rogaland Theatre, Stavanger); New Zealand (Theatre Corporate, Auckland); Yugoslavia (Modern Theatre, Belgrade)

1985   Finland (Vaasa City Theatre); Holland (Schouwburg Het Park Te Horn, Amsterdam)

1986   Iceland (Alpyduleikhusid, Reykjavik); Austria (Ensemble Theatre, Vienna)

1987   Peru (Quinta Rueda, Lima)[35]

Recent British productions

2000   Thea Sharrock Director: BAC 2 Revival (18 July–
6 August)[36]

2002   Aldwych Theatre (8 January)[37]

2006   London Academy of Music and Dramatic Art's (LAMDA)
production as part of the Royal Court's 50th Anniversary
Celebration (18–22 July)[38]

4 Workshopping the Play

The following practical exercises and discussions are intended to facilitate your exploration of *Top Girls* as a piece of theatre. Because theatre-making is such a collaborative activity, they are written out as group activities, for use by actors and students. The exercises are primarily designed to help a tutor or director conduct practical workshops on the play. However, the single reader can often easily adapt the activities to make them correspond to his or her emphasis. The creative writer could take the improvisations as creative writing prompts to begin stream of consciousness monologues or scenes. Students can especially utilize the discussions and debates to start them writing about and analysing the play. For example, to begin developing an analytical essay, you can take a conflict that interests you and write out a one- or two- sentence position. Designate two columns, labeling one 'pro' and one 'con', and then collect evidence for each position from the play itself, research, or your own logic.

Following each exercise is a series of questions to interrogate the play's larger ongoing significance, which can be utilized for essays or classroom discussions.

Group exercises and discussions

Current media images

For his 1991 revival, Max Stafford-Clark required his cast to research different images of women in the media and contrast them with 1980s images. The cast found that while women during the 1980s were portrayed as career focused, often to the exclusion of motherhood, women in 1991 were more often depicted as 'superwomen', who were expected to balance careers and children with ease.[1]

Collect recent images of women in the media and share them, then make a collage or image board to display in your study or rehearsal space. There are increasing types of media available, so pay attention to the different sources and discuss whether you consider them mainstream or alternative depictions.

Consider the following questions:

- How are career and family portrayed? How have these images changed or remained the same since the 'working woman' of the 1980s, or since the 'superwoman' of the 1990s? Are career women still portrayed as taking on masculine characteristics?
- What social classes do the women appear to belong to? What images convey their class and/or economic status? Do you find many representations of multicultural women?
- Which characters from *Top Girls* do they remind you of? Which characters from the play are most visible in the popular media? Which characters seem the most invisible?
- What other conflicts or possibilities emerge from your media images, which you feel differ from previous decades' depictions? Can you find images of men having to balance a career and family life? How often do you find images of non-nuclear and/or non-traditional families?

Thatcher debate

The play's final scene stages a condensed political argument regarding Thatcherite policies. Churchill describes how, during rehearsals, actors debated for hours the possibilities and contradictions of 'right-wing feminism'.[2] The energy of the debate between the sisters in the play ostensibly drew from the fervent political environment within the rehearsal process.

Stage a debate, with one side supporting bourgeois feminism and so arguing that Thatcher as a prime minister represented progress for women, and the other supporting socialist feminism and so claiming that Thatcher was a negative role model. You should provide historical facts to support your opinion. Present your argument to a designated judge or jury members, who will decide which side provided evidence that is more convincing and explain why. You don't necessarily have to argue or vote for what your personal opinion is, as it is often useful to understand the other side's position in an argument.

If you see fit, you can update the argument, including the role of women and minorities in politics today. For example, there are people who might disagree with Thatcher's politics but who still see her becoming prime minister as having opened doors for women in the political arena.

While the members of the 1982 cast debated the possibility of right-wing feminism, recently there have been the so-called 'Log Cabin Republicans', consisting of gay members of the US Republican party. Do you consider this to be more of a contradiction or an expression of political freedom?

Political rhetoric discussion

Respond to the following quotes, relating them to the play:

- Thatcher famously remarked: 'There is no such thing as society. There are individual men and women, and there are families.'[3]
- In 1984 Thatcher declared: 'I came to office with one deliberate intent: to change Britain from a dependent to a self-reliant society – from a give-it-to-me to a do-it-yourself nation. A get-up-and-go, instead of a sit-back-and-wait-for-it Britain.'[4]
- 'You've come a long way baby.' Virginia Slims cigarette advert.
- During the 1980s it was declared 'Greed is good.'[5] Do you

think there has been a recent return or glamorization of the 1980s?

Find a recent political speech or advertisement slogan that you find relevant to the play. Bring it in, read it to the group, and discuss.

Socialism

Churchill has acknowledged her political commitment to socialist feminism. After the fall of the Berlin Wall in 1989, and the subsequent collapse of the Soviet Union, do you think that the play should be interpreted differently?

Do you see socialism as a political possibility? Do you think the USSR and its satellite countries exemplified socialism, or do you think that overly powerful leaders corrupted the system?

Do you think that because the Royal Court was a left-leaning theatre Churchill might have been 'preaching to the converted' in the play's original production? Do you think she was aiming the play towards those who were already opposed to Thatcher's policies?

Form

The play's structure can be considered both fragmentary and circular. What connections do you see between the first act and the rest of the play? How would the play have been different if Churchill had presented the acts in a linear fashion?

Do you consider the play deterministic or open-ended? At the end of the play, do you see a possibility for change? Does the play make you want to do something about the situations presented?

Setting

The play shifts its setting from the office, considered the traditional male sphere, to the kitchen, or the traditional woman's sphere. Churchill never shows Marlene's domestic space or Joyce's working space. Why is this significant? How would you imagine Marlene's private space to be? Or Joyce's (multiple) working environments? Either draw a potential set design or write a paragraph describing the differing environments.

Class: America versus Britain
During the play, Marlene recalls her trip to America, illustrating her freedom, but also her irresponsibility.

What do you think are the differences in the distinctions between economics and class in the USA and the UK? How do you think the last scene would have been different if it were two American sisters debating Reagan's economic policies?

Why do you think the play was so well received in the USA?

Multiple-role casting
Double and triple casting provides examples of the actors' technical ability, which was praised by even those critics who criticized other aspects of the play. Perhaps most importantly for socially invested theatre, multiple-role casting can symbolize the potential for political change through the transformative power of performance. As discussed in Chapter 2, commentators have noted the parallels between many of the cross-cast characters.

Trying not to mimic the original cast list, which characters would you cross-cast, and what do you think your choices would convey to the audience? Would you try to cast opposites, showing the actor's range to the audience and emphasizing the potential for change? Or would you try to show parallels between your characters, emphasizing thematic continuity?

How much do practical considerations influence your choices? Remember that if you are staging this play with costumes you would need to provide adequate time for your actors to change.

Now compare your cast list with the original cast list.

Issues of casting and race

For the play's initial production, a white actress portrayed Lady Nijo while in the 1991 production and film, an Asian actress portrayed Nijo. In *Cloud Nine* Churchill employed cross-racial casting for a political purpose, casting a white man playing a black man to illustrate the effects of colonialism. With *Top Girls*, Churchill left the casting choice up to the director.

How do you envision casting Nijo? Would your choice of how to racially cast her affect your decisions on how to cross-cast the show? For example, would you cast Marlene and Joyce as having different racial backgrounds, although they share the same parents? The 1991 film version chose to cross-cast Nijo with Win, thereby avoiding any confusion. You might find that casting sisters from different racial or cultural groups would give different significance to the final debate scene.

Utilizing Brecht's concept of alienation, if the actress portraying Nijo remained distanced from her character instead of trying to become Nijo, would this make any difference to how the audience would understand cross-racial casting?

Production photos show that although the actress in 1982 wore a kimono, she did not make-up as a geisha; while in the film version, the actress had a full face of geisha make-up and a wig. Would such costume choices influence how you interpreted the casting? How might the different mediums of film and theatre influence such casting choices?

Do you believe in colourblind casting, or does the audience inevitably register racial difference? *Top Girls* has been praised for providing rich roles for women, so does casting by taking race into account prevent opportunities for minorities? How about the idea that the best actor should play the role regardless of race?

Although we have focused on Nijo here, there are other racial readings of the play. For instance, in the Guthrie production a black actress portrayed the waitress. What would her silence convey then? Would this necessarily confirm stereotypes, or could this be a politically informed choice?

Improvisations and practical exercises

The journalist Paul Taylor writes: 'Whenever I think about the plays of Caryl Churchill . . . I am reminded of a (. . . quote by) Ted Hughes. He wrote that the breakthroughs in art come when we manage to outwit the secret policemen in our heads.'[6] This ability strikes me as true regarding both Churchill's work and the act of improvisation, from which she gained much inspiration during her work with Joint Stock. Keeping this in mind, commit to the following improvisations, many of which deal with the power dynamics that are central to understanding Churchill's work. The first four relate to the key scene of the dinner party in Act One.

Technique: overlapping dialogue

Critical debate lingers as to the mood established by the overlapping dialogue of the play's first scene. Stafford-Clark proposes that the dinner scene's overlapping dialogue is actually quite natural. To practise overlapping dialogue, he suggests putting one actor between two other actors in a line, and then having the actors on either side of him or her talk to the central actor about completely different subjects.[7]

How does the actor respond to the split conversations? How does this ability change once you add a third conversation?

There are many ways to perform the dinner scene: here are some suggestions. First, perform the scene as though the characters are competitive and cutting each other off as acts of aggression (being mindful of your vocal chords). Next, perform the scene as though the characters are empathetic to each other's stories, and interrupting only to provide support. Finally, perform the scene as a combination of those emotions, with different lines having different tones.

Perhaps with an instructor or director's input, consider which lines are the most important for the audience to hear, and have the rest of the characters pass the right to speak to that character. (The director pointing to the character or passing an object to that character could indicate the right to speak has passed to him or her.)

The actors of the Stafford-Clark productions noted that they had to listen closely to each other's lines to hear their cues, since they are not as evident as in traditional dialogue. Pay attention to the scene's rhythm and see if you can hear if it gets thrown off at certain points.

Important silences

Lesley Sharp, who portrayed Gret in the 1991 production, considered the trauma that character would have gone through and concluded that 'Gret's silence was not that she didn't have anything to say, but that she had too much to say' (Goodman, 1989, p. 84). Keep Sharp's interpretation in mind.

When the right to speak is passed to Gret and the waitress, allow them to verbalize what they think their characters want to say. Then repeat the exercise with Gret and the waitress restraining their words. How can their desired speech be shown through their actions and expressions?

Dinner invitations

Before writing *Top Girls*, Churchill participated in a workshop with Monstrous Regiment that explored a group of women from history meeting in a 'no-man's land'.[8] Why do you think Churchill chose to depict the characters she does in the first act?

If you were able to invite a group of people to a gathering that defied the boundaries between time and space, whom would you invite? Would you invite famous people or lesser-known historical figures? Would they share a theme or political stance?

How do you think that the group dynamic would change if it included men? Where would you choose to meet? Why?

Develop a guest list and share with the group.

Age improvisation

Casting the play may well require actors to act a different age than they are, most evidently in the case of Angie and Kit. Set up an improvisation at a family gathering. Various people enter the space as characters of different ages. When a mediator enters and tags two people, they should switch ages. Then discuss how old you determined each other to be and why.

Public places

Observe strangers in public places, such as a businessperson going to work on public transport, or a group of customers and a waiter at a restaurant. Alternatively, you could visit a park or playground where you can observe children playing and interacting with their parents. You may think that you see such interactions all the time, but through this exercise, you can observe people's characteristics in a distanced manner and relate it to portrayals in the play.

Pick a simple event that you would like to convey and a person (or if you are feeling up to it, two people) who you would like to portray.

Then report back to your group. Remembering Brecht's concept of alienation, and so remaining aware of yourself as an actor, start your re-enactment: 'It happened like this', at points interrupting your act to address the audience as an actor, commenting on the action.

Interview re-enactment

Churchill interviewed people from various jobs to formulate her ideas for *Top Girls*.[9] She used a related technique during development of plays such as *Serious Money*, where actors would interview people and then report to Churchill and the collective. They would re-enact the interviews with other Joint Stock members, who would in turn become the interviewers.[10]

Depending on your role and time available, you could find it useful to interview people who share your character's vocation, economic status, or social class. Be sure to be courteous towards the person you are interviewing, informing them of the purpose of your interview. Ask respectful questions, leaving it up to the interviewee how personal the interview becomes.

Report on your findings, bringing at least two copies of the interview back to the group. Assign the role of the interviewer to another member of the group and read the transcripts aloud. Then discuss what insights you reached through the process.

Power relations and gender: card improvisation
During improvisations with Joint Stock, Churchill often used an improvisation to make societal class and gender roles more evident. Take a deck of cards and draw one: the higher the card, the higher your class and economic position. Now, interact with the group, portraying how you think that a person would move according to your status. Line up in the order that you think represents your respective card numbers and then compare cards. Repeat the exercise including improvised dialogue. Then repeat the card game with the additional factor that black cards represent male characters, and red female characters.

How close did you come to determining what card each participant drew? How did the exercise differ when including dialogue? Did dialogue make the exercise easier or more complicated?

What does participating in this exercise illustrate about power relations? How did portraying the different cards through your body and voice make you feel?

How did gender designations affect the portrayal of authority? When engaging the actors of *Cloud Nine* in a similar improvisation in 1978, Churchill found that the gender (colour) of the cards out-weighed the weight of the class and economic (number) cards, so that even if a 'male' had a low card, he was judged to have more authority than a 'woman' would. Having observed such a dynamic helps explain Churchill's depiction of characters such as Marlene, who felt that they had to 'act male' to have authority in the work-place. However, you might (hopefully) come to varying conclu-sions after your improvisations.

Re-enacting past choices

Marlene and Joyce's final scene assumes a shared history between the sisters, and depends on understanding the subtext of the lines. During the 1982 rehearsal process, the two actresses found an improvisation useful in order to find the love that the sisters had for each other, as well as their personal source of conflict.[11] Pay close attention to the references that the characters make towards their parents and childhoods. Then improvise the scene where Joyce decided to raise Marlene's child. You can include references and/or portrayals of their parents or the relevant men in their lives.

How did you reach this decision? What choices did each charac-ter make and why? How does improvising the scene change your perception of their characters?

Marlene and Joyce power switch

Switch roles between Marlene and Joyce in the final scene, paying attention to the effect that you have on the other character.

Which character do you feel more comfortable playing and why?

How do you change the way that you speak and the tones that you use? Are there points in the script where Marlene's practiced upper-class accent might be taken over by her original working-class accent?

Which character has more power at the beginning of the scene? And which at the end of the scene?

Can you think of other cases where siblings have become or been portrayed as so distant? How much of Marlene and Joyce's distance is affected by pre-established family relationships or is representative of 1980s economics?

Secrets

Stafford-Clark pointed out that one of the challenges posed by the play's structure is that audience members start to connect the plot threads rather late in the play. He reflects: 'this is a dare: you're titillating the audience by withholding information.'[12] As Harry Lane points out in 'Secrets as strategies for protection and oppression in *Top Girls*' (1998), withholding information and confessions can be seen as contrasting motifs in the play: from the job interviews, through Angie and Kit's secret, to Marlene's pregnancy and class background.

Individually, brainstorm different two-person relationships in which you think one person would have more power than the other, and write them out on strips of paper. Collect the paper strips in a bag. Get into pairs and pick a strip. Then improvise a scene where one of the characters has a secret.

In the play, how do the various power relations influence the amount of privacy allowed? How did the secrets maintain the audience's interest in the scene? Did it depend on the nature and importance of the secret?

Angie's central role

One of the ongoing secrets in the play is what Angie's notebook contains. What clues do you get and how do you imagine her notebook? Why does she keep it?

Although Churchill does not describe Angie in this manner, some reviewers have referred to Angie as 'slightly retarded'.[13] What do you think of this description? Do you think of Angie as a victim? Why or why not?

How do you understand the significance of Angie sucking Kit's menstrual blood? Would you expect audience members to squirm, laugh or be uncomfortable? How would you alleviate or heighten audience members' discomfort?

What incidents do you think finally induce Angie to travel to London? What do you think Marlene and Angie do after they leave the Top Girls agency at the end of the second act?

What effect do you think Churchill creates by Angie's enigmatic last line of 'Frightening' (141)? Do you think that Angie's fears stem from her nightmare or reality? How would you stage the end of the play to have a more personal meaning? How would you imply a broader societal connotation?

Fast-forward Angie and Kit's lives, and improvise a scene of them interacting years after the end of the play. They might have had an ongoing relationship, or have met by coincidence. What do you make of Kit's desire to become a nuclear physicist? What would their lives be like now?

Job interview

Designate an interviewer and interviewee. Send the interviewee out of the room and decide whether he or she will be considered a 'high flier' or someone who is 'not going to make it'. Then improvise a job interview of a similar length to the ones in *Top Girls*, including questions regarding educational and career credentials. If the interviewee is a 'high flyer' (101), the interviewer's objective is to convince him or her to take the job. If the person has been described as 'not going to make it', he or she can try to convince the interviewer otherwise. When it feels appropriate, an audience member or director should call out for the pair to switch roles. How long did it take for the interviewee to understand which group they were in? What signs did the interviewer provide that led to this understanding? How did the categorization affect the dynamics of the job interview? How did it feel to switch power roles?

Political interpretations

During Joint Stock rehearsals, actors were repeatedly asked to describe and act out what they thought was the political point of a scene.[14] Corresponding to Brechtian theory, this practice encourages the actor to engage not only their emotions, but their intellect as well. This also influenced Churchill's emphasis on ideas as opposed to long emotional journeys.

Take the time to discuss what you think the political point of each scene is. You may disagree with each other, with critics, or Churchill's explanation in interviews. Additionally, you might find that each scene has multiple points to make. If so, break down the scene into smaller sections and determine what you think the political point would be for each section. Then try to act out this point in your own way. How does acting out a political point differ to acting based on your character's motivation?

If you were a director or designer, what production choices might you make to clarify the political point to your audience? For instance, the last chapter included a discussion of the importance of costuming: in the dinner scene in the 1991 film version, Marlene was dressed in a blue dress, which Jane De Gay argues emphasizes her parallels with Margaret Thatcher and the Conservative party.[15] Pick a scene and make a list of different choices you would make to emphasize a political interpretation of the scene, considering elements such as costuming, set design, props, lighting and blocking.

Actioning

Stafford-Clark recommends 'actioning' one's lines, by writing a transitive verb next to each change of thought which illustrates the intent of your character's words. This process causes the actor to choose specifically how he or she is trying to affect another character. Deborah Findlay recalled that the process was particularly helpful during the dinner scene, causing the actors to decide which other characters they were trying to get to listen to different parts of their narratives. The process is most clearly expressed by an example of Findlay's notes from her 1991 script of the final scene:

(Marlene *softens* Joyce.) Marlene: Come on Joyce, what a night.
(Marlene *praises* Joyce.) You've got what it takes
(Joyce *resists* Marlene.) Joyce: I know I have
(Marlene *befriends* Joyce.) Marlene: I really didn't mean all that.
(Joyce *educates* Marlene.) Joyce: I did.[16]

Using the selection as an example, take the time to action a section of your dialogue. If you find yourself really searching for words, you could use a thesaurus, but the point is not so much finding impressive words as finding words that adequately express your intention.

Findlay portrayed Joyce in both the 1982 and 1991 productions, and found that her actioning was significantly different for each production. For instance, since Findlay wanted to be more nurturing in the later production, she took a different approach to her final line: 'No, pet. Sorry.' Instead of actioning, 'Joyce *chills* Marlene', as she did in her 1982 script, in the newer script 'Joyce *stops* and then *consoles* Marlene'.[17] The change in her choice leaves the audience with a very different impression of Joyce and Marlene's relationship.

If possible, let some time pass and return to the script. Try actioning the same section again and see if you can come up with different words. If you find that you are not affecting the other character the way you want to, how do you channel that frustration? How does the interaction change your next actioning?

5 Conclusion

This final chapter offers a speculative account of possible future productions of *Top Girls*.

I look forward to a future time when *Top Girls* can be regarded as a purely historical piece. When the 'us' vs 'them' argument at the end of the play is a reminder of civil strife resolved. When mothers and fathers are provided with childcare and equal pay and respect in the workplace. When society as a whole values domestic work along with career goals. When the narrations of patriarchal domination in the first scene will not have their parallels in the contemporary experience. When Angie's closing line of 'Frightening' rings a hollow reminder of past conflicts and inequalities.

Until then, the key to staging effective productions will be to keep aware of ongoing disparities in gender, economics and class, and to keep questioning why some reforms seem to take so long to take hold. Because in its simplest form, *Top Girls* is a call for change. Future directors and performers will think about what changes they would most like to see occur, and then highlight them in rehearsals and performance. As the discussion of multiple-role casting has indicated, potential productions could see fit to extend Churchill's critique of bourgeois feminism to include a critique of mainstream feminism's focus on white women's struggles, or to represent Britain's changing racial make-up. The sisters' relationship can indicate tensions unique to the production's locality and community make-up. Alternatively, the broad scope of the first scene could be used to emphasize the challenges that women face on the international stage.

Hopefully, future productions will not focus critique on Thatcher as a biographical figure, but keep aware of future manifestations of Thatcherism. Productions should aim to keep politicians on their toes, regardless of political party. Similarly, Marlene should not be relegated to an historical relic, but rather be viewed as representing the risks of society's ongoing emphasis on financial gain over societal and familial commitments. While the Marlenes of the future may appear to be glamorous, productions of *Top Girls* may serve to debunk the images fostered by the mainstream media. Already popular in college productions, the play can serve to educate not just in terms of historical events, but in making audience members more aware of their current situations.

Considering the play in light of Churchill's recent anti-war work has brought to mind interpretations of the play that highlight the increasingly 'frightening' international situation facing future generations. Harry Lane's reading of the play in 'Secrets as strategies for protection and oppression in *Top Girls*' seems especially insightful, drawing attention to the compromises of civil liberties that often coincide with wartime violence. His critique of Thatcher's increased state power and censorship of wartime news reports seem eerily familiar. Likewise, Kit's fear of a nuclear bomb seem newly pertinent, with North Korea's recent nuclear testing pushing the nuclear threat to the front pages in a way reminiscent of the Cold War.[1] Instead of a fanciful fort, Angie and Kit's shelter could be designed to appear more like a bomb shelter. However, their loyalty to each other and resistance to authority can now be seen as not only paralleling the Greenham Peace Camp, but also the massive protests against war in the Middle East. Perhaps, in the Brechtian fashion, productions of *Top Girls* will provide a call to action on multiple fronts.

The 'special relationship' between the USA and the UK has been the subject matter of Churchill's most recent play, and could well be explored in future productions of *Top Girls*. While in *Top Girls*

the career women describe travel to the USA, the current relationship between the two countries is considerably more fraught and
has wide-ranging ramifications. The international political landscape has become more polarized, bringing to fruition President
George W. Bush's ultimatum as a response to 9/11: 'Either you are
with us or you are with the terrorists.'[2] The current War on Terror
brings to mind Pope Joan's final words in the first act, which she
utters just prior to vomiting in a corner: 'Terrorem' (83). Linking
with Angie's more widely noted 'Frightening', Joan's terror seems
newly pertinent today.

In 1986, Britain supported the USA's bombing of Libya as retalia-
tion against terrorism. Then, as now, Churchill made her position
against retaliatory violence clear. In a telegram to the Ensemble
Theatre in Vienna she wrote a message that with minimal changes
could be sent today: 'Angry bombing of Libya. Ashamed to be
associated with the promoting of Britain's image abroad. At least
play's anti-Thatcher. Best wishes to the company.'[3]

Timeline

Politics	Society	Culture
1960s		
1962 Cuban Missile Crisis Commonwealth Immigration Act		**1962** Churchill's *The Ants* on BBC Radio 3 Formation of National Theatre Company
	1963 President John F. Kennedy assassinated The Beatles have first three hits; The Rolling Stones formed	**1963** Joan Littlewood/Theatre Workshop's *Oh, What a Lovely War!* Betty Freidan's *The Feminine Mystique* published
1964 Election of Labour Harold Wilson as prime minister		
1965 Capital punishment abolished in UK	**1965** USA offensive in Vietnam The miniskirt popularized	**1965** Edward Bond's *Saved* at the Royal Court and resulting trial
1966 General Election: Labour majority	**1966** NOW (National Organization of Women) formed in USA	**1966** Churchill's *Lovesick* (radio)

Politics	Society	Culture
1967 Abortion Act: allows termination of pregnancy with doctors' recommendations Sexual Offences Act: decriminalizes homosexuality between consenting adults		
	1968 Student uprisings in Paris and worldwide London riots in Grosvenor Square after protests against Vietnam Assassination of Robert Kennedy & Martin Luther King, Jr	**1968** Theatre censorship abolished Churchill's *Identical Twins* (radio)
1969 Voting age lowered from 21 to 18 Divorce Reform Act	**1969** Increased violence in Northern Ireland Neil Armstrong is first man on the moon	**1969** Royal Court's Theatre Upstairs established Woodstock Music Festival

Politics	Society	Culture

1970s

1970 Equal Pay Act Election of Conservative Edward Heath as prime minister

1970 Feminist protest at Miss World Contest

1970 Kate Millett's *Sexual Politics* and Germaine Greer's *The Female Eunuch* published

1971 Churchill's *Abortive* and *Not Not Not Not Not Enough Oxygen* (radio)

1972 'Bloody Sunday': direct rule of Northern Ireland begins

1972 Watergate Scandal begins in Washington DC First Miners' Strike UK unemployment passes 1 million Fuel shortages

1972 *Owners* premieres at the Royal Court Theatre

1973 Britain joins EEC (European Economic Community)

1973 USA: Roe vs Wade

1973 Almost Free Theatre Women's Festival

1974 Election of Labour Harold Wilson as prime minister

1974 National Health Service offers free family planning

1974 Founding of Joint Stock and Women's Theatre Group

1975 Margaret Thatcher elected leader of the Conservative party

1975 Saigon passes to the Communists, end of USA involvement in Vietnam

1975 Founding of Monstrous Regiment and The Women's Press

Politics	Society	Culture
1976 Harold Wilson resigns as prime minister; James Callaghan elected	**1976** High-speed Concorde planes fly from London to New York	**1976** Churchill's *Light Shining on Buckinhamshire* and *Vinegar Tom*
1978 Conservatives' campaign slogan is 'Labour Isn't Working'		
1979 'Winter of Discontent': massive strikes of public services Election of Conservative Margaret Thatcher as first female prime minister		**1979** Churchill's *Cloud Nine* Stafford-Clark appointed Artistic Director of the Royal Court Theatre

Politics	Society	Culture

1980s

1980 Republican Ronald Reagan elected US president

| | **1981** Race riots in Brixton and other urban areas | **1981** Prince Charles and Lady Diana Spencer's wedding Nell Dunn's *Steaming* |

1982 Falkland War: Argentina invades the Falkland Islands, Britain recaptures them: Thatcher's popularity at a high

1982 Greenham Common Women's Peace Camp formed British unemployment over 3 million US Equal Rights Amendment fails

1982 Churchill's *Top Girls* premieres at the Royal Court Theatre

1983 General Election: Conservative majority

1983 Churchill's *Fen.* Sarah Daniels' *Masterpieces*, debate over pornography ensues

1984 IRA bomb attempts to assassinate Thatcher Reagan re-elected US president

1984 Greenham Common cleared by police Miners' Strike

1984 Madonna's 'Material Girl' released

1985 Mikhail Gorbachev becomes leader of USSR

1985 Live Aid rock festival to provide famine relief to Africa

Politics	Society	Culture
1986 US raid on Libya	**1986** Chernobyl nuclear disaster in USSR	
1987 Conservatives re-elected	**1987** 'Black Monday': stock exchange falls, allegations of illegal share dealing at Guinness AIDS crisis intensifies	**1987** Churchill's *Serious Money*
1988 Cuts on income tax George Bush elected US president	**1988** Airplane explosion over Lockerbie, Scotland	**1988** Timberlake Wertenbaker's *Our Country's Good*
1989 Nigel Lawson, Chancellor of the Exchequer, resigns	**1989** Tiananmen Square massacre Fall of the Berlin Wall	

Politics	Society	Culture

1990s

1990   Thatcher resigns as prime minister; John Major (Conservative) replaces her

1990   Trafalgar Square riot against the Poll Tax

1990   Churchill's *Mad Forest*

1991   Susan Faludi's *Backlash: The Undeclared War Against Women* published

1991   Stafford-Clark revival of *Top Girls* at the Royal Court Filming of Open University/BBC version of *Top Girls*

Notes

Chapter 1

1 Churchill, C. (1960) 'Not ordinary, not safe', *The Twentieth Century*. November, p. 448, cited in Aston, 2001 p. 80.

2 Nightingale 1991.

3 Ravenhill 1997, p. 14.

4 Aston 2001, p. 1.

5 Churchill quoted in Thurman, J. (1982) 'The playwright who makes you laugh about orgasm, racism, class struggle, homophobia, woman-hating, the British empire, and the irrepressible strangeness of the human heart', *Ms*. p.54. Cited in Aston 2001, p. 4.

6 Aston 2001, p. 4.

7 Churchill, C. (1960) 'Not ordinary, not safe', cited in Aston, 2001, p. 80.

8 Theodore Shank provides a break down of the educational background common to many London playwrights. 1994, pp. 183–4.

9 Interview with Helene Keyssar, March 1982. Cited in Keyssar 1984, pp. 79–80.

10 Churchill quoted by Gussow 1987, p. 26.

11 Coined by Carol Hanisch and used by writers such as Kate Millett, who were influential during the 1970s.

12 Itzin 1980, p. 282.

13 Chambers, C. and Prior, M. (1987) *Playwright's Progress: Patterns of Postwar British Drama*. Oxford: Amber Land Press. Cited by Goodman 1993, p. 92.

14 McFerran 1977, p. 13.

15 Ibid., p. 15.

16 Itzin 1980, p. 274.

17 Churchill cited in Itzin 1980, p. 285.

18 Although Churchill is the sole author of *Vinegar Tom*, Churchill co-wrote *Floorshow* with the playwrights Byrony Lavery, Michelene Wandor and David Bradford. Itzin 1980, p. 277.

19   Rich refers to *Fen* as 'Bottom Girls' (1983a) while Aston refers to the play
      as 'Land Girls' (2001, p. 64).

20   Churchill 1990c.

21   For instance, recently the playwrights April de Angelis, Stella Feehily, and
      Laura Wade explained how much Churchill's work continues to mean to
      them. See Edwardes 2006.

22   Aston 2001, p. 15.

23   For instance, see Elaine Aston's interview with Gillian Hanna, who is one
      of the founders of Monstrous Regiment. Hanna compares Churchill's
      career path with Monstrous Regiment's and expresses her admiration for
      Churchill's ongoing innovation during a period which has proven diffi-
      cult for most feminist playwrights. Aston 1997, p. 71.

24   Rowbotham 1997, pp. 401–2.

25   Ibid., pp. 378–9.

26   Goodman 1993, p. 66.

27   Betsko and Koenig 1987, p. 77.

28   Austin 1990, p. 6. For further descriptions of feminisms, see Wandor
      1981, p. 134, and Dolan 1988, pp. 3–6.

29   Keyssar 1984, xiii.

30   Rowbotham 1997, p. 449.

31   Ibid., p. 405.

32   Ibid., p. 415.

33   Stevenson 2004, p. 39.

34   Toufexis 1982.

35   Bidder 1985.

36   Rowbotham 1997, p. 495.

37   Betsko and Koenig 1987, p. 78.

38   Ibid.

39   See 'An interview with Thatcher' 1979.

40   Rowbotham 1997, p. 491.

41   For interviews illustrating the range of the British public's memories
      regarding Thatcher, see 'Thatcher's children' (2000), the subtitle claims:
      'They loved her, they loathed her, they were made by her, they were
      broken by her. And 10 years after she was ousted from power, they've
      never forgotten her.'

42   Budge et al. 1998, pp. 76–7.

43   Riddell 1989, p. 12.

44   Rowbotham p. 479.

45   Budge et al. 1998, p. 77.

46   Rowbotham 1997, p. 479.

47   Ibid., p. 491.

48 Ibid., p. 412.
49 Riddell 1989, p. 158.
50 Scott, J. (1997) *British Social Attitudes: The 13th Report*. Dartmouth: Aldershott, cited in Leonard 1997, p. 25.
51 Schalch 2006.
52 'Testimony' 1947.
53 Rowbotham, pp. 480–1.

Chapter 2

 1 Churchill quoted in Goodman 1998, p. 72.
 2 Betsko and Koenig 1987, p. 82.
 3 Chicago 1979, p. 139.
 4 Brazell 1973a, p. xix.
 5 Ibid., p. xvi.
 6 Ibid., p. viii.
 7 Bird quoted in Barr 1970, p. 116.
 8 The Project Gutenberg and the Victorian Women Writers Project have collected Bird's writings. For the full text of 'A lady's life in the Rocky Mountains', see 'Collected travel writings of Isabella Bird'.
 9 Chicago 1979, p. 139.
10 *Looking for Pope Joan*, 2005.
11 Translated by Dr. Peter Glare, St. Cross College. Cited in Godiwala 2003, p. 10. For a full translation, see the opening of Book II in the 'Internet Classics Archive', <http://classics.mit.edu/Carus/nature_things.2.ii.html>
12 Rubik cites from a lecture by Jutta Thellmann (1996, pp. 180–1).
13 Christopher Brown, *Brueghel*. Phaidon, 1975. Cited in Griffiths 1993, p. 157, n. 9.
14 For a description of the children's fate, see Chaucer, p. 337. Giovanni Boccaccio's version included in his *Decameron* (c. 1353) is available at: http://classiq.net/giovanni-boccaccio/the-story-of-griselda/index.html. For Francesco Petrarch's version in translation, see: 'Petrarch: the Tale of Griselda", <http://petrarch.petersadlon.com/griselda.html>
15 Ritchie 1987, pp. 11–12.
16 Churchill describes the workshopping process in Ritchie 1987, p. 119.
17 Gaskill 1988, p. 135.
18 Churchill interviewed by Lynne Truss in 'A fair cop', *Plays and Players*, January 1984, pp. 9–10. Cited in Fitzsimmons 1989, p. 61.
19 Gaskill 1988, p. 59.
20 Churchill in a letter to Janelle Reinelt, 23 February 1985. Cited in Reinelt 1996, p. 86.

21 Victoria Radin, 'Churchill's Adventures', *Sunday Observer* (Review/ Arts) 15 August 1989: 29. Cited in Kritzer 1991, p. 208 n. 1.

22 'Alienation effects in Chinese acting', Brecht 1957, p. 91. Also see 'A short organum for the theatre', Brecht 1957, pp. 121–9.

23 'A short organum for the theatre', in Brecht 1957, p. 190.

24 'Alienation effects in the narrative pictures of the Elder Brueghel', in Brecht 1957, pp. 157–8.

25 Budge et al.1998, p. 401.

26 Betsko and Koenig 1987, p. 79.

27 Both journalists and scholars have considered the play postmodern. See Gardner 2002 and Pankratz 1999, p. 177.

28 For a theoretical exploration of postmodernity's relation to universal narratives, see Jean-Francois Lyotards' *The Postmodern Condition*.

29 For further analysis of the relationship between feminism and postmodernism, see Reinelt 1996, p. 84.

30 Gussow 1987, p. 27.

31 Aston and Brown both agree with Cohn and Rubik's perception of the dinner scene's characters as self-centered.

32 Lane 1998, p. 64.

33 See Barrow 2006 for an example.

34 Goodman 1998, p. 97.

35 'Post-feminism' was a term originally coined by the journalist Susan Bolotin in 1982 (Rowbotham 1997, p. 543).

36 Hartley-Brewer 1999, p. 6.

37 See Long 1998, pp. 103–8.

38 Such exceptions include Rebecca Prichard's premiere *Essex Girls* (1994). Prichard recalled that her decision to shift the times depicted in her first and second act was influenced by Churchill's experimentations in form. Prichard quoted in Sierz 2000, p. 226.

39 Ravenhill in Edgar 1999, p. 50.

40 Komporaly 2006, p. 53.

41 Innes 2002, p. 519. For the Pope's speech, see Churchill 1990a, p. 83.

Chapter 3

1 Stafford-Clark was part of a discussion panel at the National's 2000 reading of *Top Girls* which reunited the original cast members (Stafford-Clark 2007, p. 211).

2 Churchill 1990c.

3 Manville quoted in Goodman 1998, p. 73.

4 Stafford-Clark 2007, p. 102.

5 Rumens, C. (1982) 'The price of success', *Times Literary Supplement*,

24 September, p. 1035. Cited in Fitzsimmons 1989, p. 57.

6   Churchill quoted in Keyssar 1994, p. 100.

7   Correspondence between Churchill and Huber, 2 April 1986. The Vienna premiere occurred at the Ensemble Theatre directed by Peter Gruber. Cited in Fitzsimmons 1989, pp. 63–4.

8   Aston 2003, p. 23.

9   Logan, B. (2000) 'Review of Caryl Churchill's *Top Girls*', *The Independent*, 21 May. Included in *Theatre Record,* p. 930.

10 See the following reviews: Halliburton, R. (2000) 'Review of Caryl Churchill's *Top Girls*', *The Evening Standard*, 19 July. Included in *Theatre Record*, p. 930; North, M. (2000) 'Review of Caryl Churchill's *Top Girls*', *Time Out*, 26 July. Included in *Theatre Record*, p. 931.

11 Churchill 1990a, p. 54.

12 Gardner, L. (2000) 'Review of Caryl Churchill's *Top Girls*', *The Guardian*, 21 July. Included in *Theatre Record*, p. 931.

13 Nightingale 1991.

14 Logan 2000, p. 930.

15 Stafford-Clark quoted in Goodman 1998, p. 76.

16 Goodman 1998, p. 88.

17 *Plays and Players*. November 1982, p. 23.

18 Rossenstein 2002.

19 Rich 1982, p. 59.

20 Stone, L. (1983) 'Making room at the top', *The Village Voice*, XXVII, 9. 1 March, p. 81. Cited in Fitzsimmons 1989, p. 61.

21 Interview with the director Jo Bonney by dramaturg Diana Konopka, Williamstown Theater Festival programme 20–31 July 2005, p. 28.

22 Godiwala 2003, p. 189 n. 145.

23 For a review, see Weir 2003. For production photos, see 'The Guthrie Theater – Top Girls Proofsheet'.

24 Quoted in Goodman 1998, p. 69.

25 Betsko and Koenig 1987, p. 82.

26 Rossenstein 2002.

27 Logan 2000, p. 930.

28 De Gay 1998, p. 103; Nunn 2002, p. 169.

29 Churchill and Stafford-Clark quoted in Goodman 1998, pp. 91–2.

30 Manville quoted in Goodman 1998, p. 89.

31 De Gay 1998, p. 106.

32 Stafford-Clark quoted in Goodman 1998, p. 93.

33 Churchill 1990a, p. 53.

34 For a list of the cast, see Rich 1983b. Rich prefers the British ensemble, though noting the American standout performances of Linda Hunt and Valerie Mahaffey.

35 Fitzsimmons 1989, pp. 8–9.
36 See *Theatre Record* 2000, p. 930.
37 Gardner 2002.
38 The Royal Court Theatre website, <www.theroyalcourttheatre.com>

Chapter 4
1 Lesley Manville quoted in Goodman 1998, pp. 77–8.
2 Kritzer 1991, p. 139.
3 Thatcher interview in Keay 1987.
4 Thatcher made this comment in a speech at a Small Business Bureau Conference on 8 February, 1984. Gardner found this quote to be especially relevant in her 2002 review of *Top Girls.*
5 Michael Douglas as Gordon Gekko in *Wall Street* (1987).
6 Taylor 2006.
7 Stafford-Clark quoted by Goodman 1998, p. 81.
8 This workshop occurred at the Institute of Contemporary Arts in London during the 1970s and theatre historian Keith Peacock speculates that it may have contributed to Churchill's conception of *Top Girls'* first act. (1999, p. 94).
9 Churchill quoted by Goodman 1998, p. 72.
10 Max Stafford-Clark 2007, p. 129.
11 Deborah Findlay quoted by Goodman 1998, p. 74.
12 Stafford-Clark quoted by Goodman 1998, p. 79.
13 Sternlicht 2005, p. 101.
14 William Gaskill quoted in Itzin 1980, p. 221.
15 De Gay 1998, p. 106.
16 For the dialogue in *Top Girls*, see p. 141.
17 For the excerpt from Findlay's script, see Goodman 1998, pp. 86–7.

Chapter 5
1 For an example of recent conflicts, see 'North Korea pledges to test nuclear bomb', 4 October 2006 <http://www.cnn.com/2006/WORLD/asiapcf/10/03/nkorea.nuclear/index>
2 'Transcript of President Bush's Address', 20 September 2002 <http://archives.cnn.com/2001/US/09/20/gen.bush.transcript/>
3 Telegram dated 17 April 1986. Quoted in Fitzsimmons 1989, p. 64.

Further Reading

Print

Aston, E. (2001) *Caryl Churchill: Writers and Their Work.* Estover, Plymouth: Northcote. As part of her book on Churchill's body of work, Aston brings attention to the 'us vs them' mentality articulated in *Top Girls*.

Aston, E. (2003) *Feminist Views on the English Stage: Women Playwrights, 1990–2000.* Cambridge: Cambridge University Press, pp. 18–36. Aston's chapter on Churchill addresses the 1991 revival of *Top Girls* and its ongoing importance to a new generation of women playwrights.

Buse, P. (2002) 'Towards a citational history – Churchill with Benjamin', in *Drama & Theory: Critical Approaches to Modern British Drama.* Manchester: Manchester University Press, pp. 111–29. In this chapter, Buse examines *Top Girls* in light of Walter Benjamin's philosophy of history.

Cousin, G. (1989) *Churchill: The Playwright.* London: Methuen. Spans Churchill's works through the 1980s.

Dunn, N. (1981) *Steaming.* Derbyshire: Amber Lane. This play is often used as a comparison to *Top Girls* because it was a successful all-woman production of the same period. However, *Steaming* is written from a more bourgeois feminist perspective and illustrates woman's commonalities as opposed to their differences.

Fitzsimmons, L. (1987) '"I won't turn back for you or anyone": Caryl Churchill's socialist-feminist theatre', *Essays in*

Theatre 6(1), November, 19–29. An insightful early essay comparing the plays *Top Girls* and *Fen*, this defines the different types of feminism during the 1980s, favouring socialist feminism. Fitzsimmons also considers some of the textual changes that Churchill made in her final published version of the play.

Fitzsimmons, L. (ed.) (1989) *File on Churchill*. London: Methuen. Compiles a selection of interview clips and critics' responses to Churchill's plays until 1988.

Godiwala, D. (2003) *Breaking the Bounds: British Feminist Dramatists Writing in the Mainstream Since c.1980*. New York: Lang, pp. 8–16, 40–52. Includes criticism of the racial politics in Churchill's works. Influenced by the theoretical work of Michel Foucault.

Goodman, L. (1993) *Contemporary Feminist Theatres: To Each Her Own*. London: Routledge, pp. 90–4. Discusses Churchill's collaboration with Joint Stock and Monstrous Regiment as part of Goodman's examination of feminist theatres' working methods.

Keyssar, H. (1984) *Feminist Theatre: An Introduction to Plays of Contemporary British and American Women*. London: Macmillan, pp. 77–101. In this initial work on Churchill, Keyssar pays special attention to Churchill's writing process and cites from initial reviews, which often perceived of *Top Girls* as confusing.

Kritzer, A. H. (1991) *The Plays of Caryl Churchill: Theatre of Empowerment*. New York: St Martin's Press. Examines *Top Girl's* politics, contrasting what Kritzer terms the 'ethic of caring' and 'ethic of competition'.

Nunn, H. (2002) *Thatcher, Politics and Fantasy: The Political Culture of Gender and Nation*. London: Lawrence & Wishart. A scholarly, in-depth look at Thatcher's persona and representation of gender.

Rabillard, S. (ed.) (1998) *Caryl Churchill: Contemporary Re-Presen-*

tations. Winnipeg: Blizzard. This most recent collection on Churchill includes chapters on the 1991 BBC video production of *Top Girls*, and a chapter considering the play in light of the secrecy surrounding the Falklands War.

Randall, P. R. (ed.) (1988) *Caryl Churchill: A Casebook.* New York: Garland. In this initial collection on Churchill, the play is viewed in the context of the feminist arguments of the day, which opposed patriarchy and called for a shift from an emphasis on personal autonomy to societal transformation.

Reinelt, J. (1996) *After Brecht: British Epic Theater.* Ann Arbor: University of Michigan Press, pp. 81–92. Focuses on the Brechtian influences in Churchill's plays and relates her work to socialist feminism.

Reinelt, J. (2000) 'Caryl Churchill and the politics of style', in E. Aston and J. Reinelt (eds), *The Cambridge Companion to Modern British Women Playwrights.* Cambridge: Cambridge University Press, pp. 174–94. Reinelt focuses on Churchill's work as stemming from the political tensions of the Thatcher era, also including more recent productions.

Rowbotham, S. (1997) *A Century of Women: The History of Women in Britain and the United States.* London: Viking. Rowbotham's history focuses on the story of middle- and lower-class women, instead of the more commonly visible upper class. She substantiates Churchill's claims that while Margaret Thatcher provided a figurehead of female power, her policies detrimentally affected working-class women.

Thomas, J. (1992) 'The plays of Caryl Churchill: essays in refusal', in A. Page (ed.), *The Death of the Playwright?* Basingstoke: Macmillan, pp. 160–85. If you are interested in the power relations that Churchill depicts, this essay – an in-depth literary analysis of *Top Girls* and *Cloud Nine* based on the work of Michel Foucault – will be interesting.

Non-print

Approaching Top Girls (1995) Open University BBC. This film adaptation of the play includes interviews with Churchill, Stafford-Clark and many of the actors from the Royal Court productions, as well as an introductory analysis by Lizbeth Goodman.

Looking for Pope Joan (2005) ABC News: Primetime. 29 December. www.abcnews.go.com/Primetime/story?id=1453197&page=1 (accessed 27 March 2007). This website includes a clip of the recent ABC report tracking the debate surrounding Pope Joan.

www.theroyalcourttheatre.com The Royal Court website, providing a history of the theatre and a performance archive that includes reviews and pictures of recent Churchill productions.

References

'An interview with Thatcher', *Time*, 14 May 1979.

Aston, E. (1997) (ed.) *Feminist Theatre Voices.* Loughborough: Loughborough Theatre Texts.

Austin, G. (1990) *Feminist Theories for Dramatic Criticism.* Ann Arbor: University of Michigan Press.

Barr, P. (1970) *A Curious Life for a Lady: the Story of Isabella Bird.* Leicestershire: Charnwood.

Barrow, B. (2006) 'Hard times for "Thatcher's Children"', *Daily Mail*, 17 October.

Benedict, D. (1997) 'The mother of reinvention', *Independent*, 9 April, p. 4.

Betsko, K. and Koenig, R. (1987) *Interviews with Contemporary Women Playwrights.* New York: Beech Tree Books, pp. 75–84. (This includes Churchill interviewed by the editors on 25 February 1984, and by the playwright Emily Mann on 23 November 1984.)

Bidder, J. (1985) 'Who's playing fair?', *The London Sunday Times*, 29 September.

Bimberg, C. (1997) 'Caryl Churchill's *Top Girls* and Timberlake Wertenbaker's *Our Country's Good* as contributions to a definition of culture', *Connotations*, 7(3), 399–416.

Brazell, K. (1973a) 'Introduction', *The Confessions of Lady Nijo.* New York: Doubleday.

Brazell, K. (1973b) (trans.) *The Confessions of Lady Nijo.* New York: Doubleday.

Brecht, B. (1957) *Brecht on Theatre: The Development of an Aesthetic.* J. Willett (ed. and trans.). New York: Hill and Wang.

Brewer, M. (1999) *Race, Sex and Gender in Contemporary Women's Theatre.* Brighton: Sussex Academic Press.

Brown, J. (1988) 'Caryl Churchill's *Top Girls* catches the next wave', in P. Randall (ed.), *Caryl Churchill: A Casebook.* London: Garland Press, pp. 117–31.

Budge, I., Crewe, I., McKay, D. and Newton, K. (1998) *The New British Politics.* New York: Addison Wesley Longman, Inc.

Case, S. (1988) *Feminism and Theatre.* New York: Methuen.

Chaucer, G. *The Canterbury Tales.* P. Tuttle (2006) (trans.) New York: Barnes and Noble.

Chicago, J. (1979) *The Dinner Party: A Symbol of Our Heritage.* Garden City, New York: Anchor Books.

Churchill, C. (1990a) *Top Girls. Caryl Churchill Plays: 2.* London: Methuen.

Churchill, C. (1990b) 'Introduction', *Caryl Churchill Plays: 2.* London: Methuen.

Churchill, C. (1990c) 'Introduction', *Churchill: Shorts.* London: Nick Hern.

Cohn, R. (1991) 'Splitting images of the mind', in *Retreats from Realism in Recent English Drama.* Cambridge: Cambridge University Press, pp. 128–60.

'Collected travel writings of Isabella Bird', *Genesha Publishing Ltd.* <www.ganesha-publishing.com/bird_intro> (accessed 27 March 2007).

D'Arcy, C.C.G. (1995) '"The personal is political" in Caryl Churchill's *Top Girls*: a parable for the feminist movement in Thatcher's Britain', in S. Onega (ed.), *Telling Histories: Narrativizing History, Historicizing Literature.* Atlanta, Georgia: Rodopi, pp. 103–15.

De Gay, J. (1998) 'Colour me beautiful? Clothes consciousness in the Open University/BBC video production of *Top Girls*', in S. Rabillard (ed.), *Caryl Churchill: Contemporary Re-Presentations.* Winnipeg: Blizzard, pp. 102–14.

Diamond, E. (1997) *Unmaking Mimesis: Essays on Feminism and Theater*. New York: Routledge.

Dolan, J. (1988) *The Feminist Spectator as Critic*. Ann Arbor: University of Michigan Press.

Edgar, D. (1999) *State of Play: Playwrights on Playwriting*. London: Faber.

Edwardes, J. (2006) 'Celebrating Caryl Churchill', *Time Out*, 14 November.

Gardner, L. (2002) 'Material girls: Caryl Churchill's *Top Girls* summed up the 1980s ethos of ambition, ego and greed. As the play hits the West End 20 years after its premiere, Lyn Gardner finds that little has changed', *Guardian*, 2 January.

Gaskill, W. (1988) *A Sense of Direction*. London: Faber.

Goodman, L. (1998) 'Overlapping dialogue in overlapping media: behind the scenes of *Top Girls*', in S. Rabillard (ed.), *Caryl Churchill: Contemporary Re-Presentations*. Winnipeg: Blizzard, pp. 69–102.

Griffiths, T. R. (1993) 'Waving not drowning, the mainstream 1979–88', in T.R. Griffiths and M. Llewellyn-Jones (eds), *British and Irish Women Dramatists Since 1958*. Buckingham, England: Open University Press, pp. 47–77.

Gussow, M. (1987) 'Genteel playwright, angry voice', *New York Times*, 22 November.

'The Guthrie Theater – Top Girls Proofsheets' <www.proofsheet. com/guthrie/girls/> (accessed on 12 May 2007).

Hartley-Brewer, J. (1999) 'Brave new age dawns for single women', *Guardian*, 18 October, p. 6.

Innes, C. (2002) *Modern British Drama: The Twentieth Century*. Cambridge: Cambridge University Press.

Itzin, C. (1980) *Stages in the Revolution: Political Theatre in Britain since 1968*. London: Methuen.

Keay, D. (1987) 'AIDS, education and the year 2000', *Woman's Own*, 31 October.

Komporaly, J. (2006) *Staging Motherhood: British Women Playwrights, 1965 to the Present*. Houndmills, Basingstroke, Hampshire: Palgrave.

Lane, H. (1998) 'Secrets as strategies for protection and oppression in *Top Girls*', in S. Rabillard (ed.), *Caryl Churchill: Contemporary Re-Presentations*. Winnipeg: Blizzard, pp. 60–9.

Leonard, M. (1997) *Britain [TM]: Rediscovering Our Identity*. London: Redwood.

Long, J. (1998) 'What share of the cake now? The employment of women in the English theatre (1994)', in L. Goodman and J. de Gay (eds), *The Routledge Reader in Gender and Performance*. London: Routledge, pp. 103–8.

Marx, K. and Engels, F. (1935) *The Communist Manifesto*, in E. Burns (ed.), *A Handbook of Marxism*. London: Victor Gollancz, pp. 21–60.

McFerran, A. (1977) 'The theatre's (somewhat) angry young women', *Time Out*, 28 –30 November, p. 13.

Merrill, L. (1988) 'Monsters and heroines: Caryl Churchill's women', in P. Randall (ed.), *Caryl Churchill: A Casebook*. London: Garland Press, pp. 71–91.

Nightingale, B. (1991) 'Emancipation chiller', *The London Times*, 16 April.

Pankratz, A. (1999) 'Perceiving and performing Caryl Churchill: the drama of gender construction', in Ursula Pasero and Friederike Braun (eds), *Wahrnehmung und Herstellung von Geschlect: Perceiving and Performing Gender*. Opladen: Westdeutscher Verlag, pp. 177–87.

Peacock, K. (1999) *Thatcher's Theatre: British Theatre and Drama in the Eighties*. London: Greenwood Press.

Ravenhill, M. (1997) 'Dramatic moments', *Guardian*, 9 April, p. 14.

Rich, F. (1982) 'Caryl Churchill's *Top Girls* at the Public', *New York Times*, 29 December.

Rich, F. (1983a) '*Fen,* new work by Caryl Churchill', *New York Times*, 31 May.

Rich, F. (1983b) '*Top Girls* gets a new American cast', *New York Times*, 17 March.

Riddell, P. (1989) *The Thatcher Decade: How Britain Has Changed during the 1980s.* Oxford: Basil Blackwell.

Ritchie, R. (1987) *The Joint Stock Book: The Making of a Theatre Collective.* London: Methuen.

Rosefeldt, P. (1995) 'The father and the invisible patriarchy: Caryl Churchill's *Top Girls*', *The Absent Father in Modern Drama,* Series III, Comparative Literature Vol. 54. New York: Peter Lang, pp. 127–35.

Rossenstein, B. (2002) 'Nearly topflight', *San Francisco Bay Guardian*, 12 June.

Rubik, M. (1996) 'The silencing of women in feminist British drama', in G.M. Grabher and U. Jessner (eds), *Semantics of Silences in Linguistics and Literature*, Heidelburg: Universitatsverlag C. Winter, pp. 177–90.

Schalch, K. (2006) '1981 strike leaves legacy for American workers', <www.npr.org/templates/story/story.php?storyId=5604656> (accessed 6 March 2007).

Schneider, M. (2004) 'Deviant speech: understanding Churchill's use of feminine linguistics in *Top Girls*', in S. Constantinidis (ed.), *Text & Presentation.* London: McFarland & Company, Inc., pp. 144–57.

Shank, T. (1994) *Contemporary British Theatre.* London: Macmillan.

Sierz, A. (2001) *In-Yer-Face Theatre: British Drama Today.* London: Faber.

Stafford-Clark, M. (2007) *Taking Stock: The Theatre of Max Stafford-Clark.* London: Nick Hern.

Sternlicht, S. (2005) *Masterpieces of Modern British and Irish Drama.* Westport, CT: Greenwood Press.

Stevenson, R. (2004) *The Last of England?* The Oxford English

Literary History. Vol. 12, 1960–2000. Oxford: Oxford University Press.

Taylor, P. (2006) 'One of a kind', *Independent*, 16 November.

'Testimony of Ronald Reagan before HUAC', 23 October 1947. <www.cnn.com/SPECIALS/cold.war/episodes/06/documents/huac/reagan> (accessed 10 March 2007).

'Thatcher's children', *Independent*, 21 November 2000.

Theatre Record (2000) Reviews of *Top Girls* by Caryl Churchill. Directed by Thea Sharrock. 18 July–6 August, pp. 930–1.

Toufexis, A. (1982) 'What killed equal rights?', *Time*, 12 July.

Wandor, M. (1981) *Carry On Understudies: Theatre and Sexual Politics*. London: Routledge.

Weir, E. (2003) 'Minneapolis', *Talkin' Broadway*. <www.Talkin-Broadway.Org>, Inc. 27 May.

Whelehan, I. (2000) *Overloaded: Popular Culture and the Future of Feminism*. London: The Women's Press.

Timeline information

Aston, E. and Reinelt, J. (eds) (2000) *The Cambridge Companion to Modern British Women Playwrights*. Cambridge: Cambridge University Press, pp. xvi–xix.

Mercer, D. (ed.) (1996) *Chronicle of the World*. New York: DK Publishing Inc., pp. 1052–109.

Morgan, K. (ed.) (1998) *The Oxford Popular History of Britain*. Oxford: Oxford University Press.

Rowbotham, S. (1997) *A Century of Women: The History of Women in Britain and the United States*. London: Viking.

Shellard, D. (1999) *British Theatre Since the War*. New Haven: Yale University, pp. xiii–xix.

Index

'actioning' 98–9
air traffic controllers' strike (1981)
    22
  see also trade unions
alienation effect
  see Brecht, Bertolt
Amato, Bianca 81
Angelis, April de 114n. 21
anti-war beliefs 22, 70, 102–3
Aristotelian-based theatre 42
Armstrong, Neil 106
Aston, Elaine 15, 60, 63, 66

Beatles, The 105
Beckett, Samuel 8
Benedict, David 41
Berlin wall, fall of 88, 110
Bimberg, Christiane 64
Bird, Isabella (as historical figure)
    23–5, 29, 38
Blair, Tony 13
Boccaccio, Giovanni 39
  Decameron 115n. 14
Bolotin, Susan 116n. 35
Bond, Edward
  Saved 7, 105
Bradford, David
  Floorshow 113n. 18
Brecht, Bertolt 41–4, 65, 90, 93,
    98, 102
  alienation effect 42–3, 90, 93
  Berliner Ensemble 41

epic theatre 42
gestus 42–3
historicization 42–3
Mother Courage 41
Brewer, Mary 64–5
  Race, Sex, and Gender in Contem-
    porary Women's Theatre 64
Bonney, Jo 76
Brown, Janet 67
Brueghel, Pieter the Elder 24, 39
  'Dulle Griet' 29–30, 39, 43–4
Bush, George 110
Bush, George W. 13, 103

Cadell, Selina 83
Callaghan, James 108
capitalism 2, 10, 13, 18, 37, 44,
    46, 56–7, 65–6
career ladder 21, 46, 55
career woman 2, 5, 11, 23, 29, 34,
    52, 74, 78, 86, 103
  'new woman' 21
  'superwoman' 52, 86
  working woman 4, 21, 64, 78,
    86
Case, Sue-Ellen 16
censorship 7, 70, 102
Chaucer, Geoffrey 39
  Canterbury Tales, The 24, 31,
    115n. 14
Chicago, Judy
  Dinner Party, The 37

childcare 6, 74, 101
Churchill, Caryl biography 4–13
　Abortive 107
　Ants, The 7
　*Blue Heart: Heart's Desire, Blue
　　Kettle* 12
　Cloud Nine 10, 90, 94, 108
　Downstairs 5
　Drunk Enough to say I Love You?
　　13
　Far Away 12–13
　Fen 10, 109
　Floorshow 9, 113n. 18
　Having a Wonderful Time 5
　Hotel 12
　Icecream 12
　Identical Twins 106
　'Iraq.doc' 12
　Judge's Wife, The 7
　Legion Hall Bombing, The 7
　Light Shining in Buckinghamshire
　　9–10, 108
　Lives of the Great Poisoners 12
　Lovesick 105
　Mad Forest 111
　*Not Not Not Not Not Enough
　　Oxygen* 107
　Number, A 11
　Objections to Sex and Violence 8
　Owners 7
　radio plays (BBC) 7–8, 105–7
　Serious Money 10–11, 93–4, 110
　Skriker, The 11
　Softcops 11
　This Is a Chair 12
　Three More Sleepless Nights 10
　Vinegar Tom 9, 43
　You've no Need to Be Frightened 5
Churchill, Robert 5
class conflict 2, 4, 13, 16–18, 20,

37, 43–4, 55–7, 59, 75–8,
81–2, 86, 89, 94–6, 101
　'us versus them' 18, 56–7, 72,
　　101
　see also working class community
Cohn, Ruby 68
　*Retreats from Realism in Recent
　　English Drama* 61
Cold War 16, 102, 105
　see also USSR
Communism 22, 40
Conservative party 44, 56, 76, 81,
　　98, 107–11
　right wing 2, 13, 17–18,
　　86–7
　see also Thatcher, Margaret

Daniels, Sarah
　Masterpieces 8, 109
D'Arcy, Chantal Cornut-Gentille
　64
De Gay, Jane 68, 81, 98
Democratic party 81
Diamond, Elin 43, 63
Dunn, Nell
　Steaming 109

employment agency setting 25, 28,
　　36, 45–6, 49–51, 56
　interviews 26–7, 34–5, 96–7
Engels, Friedrich
　The Communist Manifesto 18
　see also Marx, Karl
epic theatre
　see Brecht, Bertolt
Equal Pay Act 17, 107
Equal Rights Amendment, 17, 109
European Economic Community
　　(EEC) 107

Falkland War 109
Faludi, Susan
  *Backlash: The Undeclared War
    Against Woman* 111
Feehily, Stella 114n. 21
feminism 8, *13–17*, 19, 33–4, 45,
    63–4, 67–8, 70, 76, 86–8, 101
  American 14–17
  backlash against 64, 67, 111
  bourgeois 15–18, 45, 63–4, 87,
    101
  British 14–17, 19
  first wave 13
  'new' 68
  post-feminism 4, 67, 116n. 35
  radical 15–16
  right wing 86–7
  second wave 13, 33–4
  socialist, materialist 15–17,
    63–4, 74, 87–8
  third wave 67
Findlay, Deborah 83, 98–9
Fitzsimmons, Linda 62–3
Foucault, Michel
  Discipline and Punish 11
Freidan, Betty
  The Feminine Mystique 105

Gardner, Lyn 74
Gaskill, William 41
gender 2, 10, 15–16, 20, 30, 35,
    43, 45–6, 49, 61, 64–5, 67–8,
    74, 79, 94–5, 101
  see also feminism
gestus
  see Brecht, Bertolt
'glass ceiling' 17, 49, 51, 79
  see also sexism, career woman
Godiwala, Dimple 3, 77
Goodman, Lizbeth 4, 66, 79

Gorbachev, Mikhail 109
Greenham Common Women's
    Peace Camp 22, 70, 102, 109
Greer, Germaine 69
  Female Eunuch 69, 107
Gruber, Peter 117n. 7

Hanisch, Carol 113n. 11
Hanna, Gillian 114n. 23
  see also Monstrous Regiment
Hare, David
  Fanshen 40
Harter, David 6–7
Hartwell, Peter 83
Hayman, Carole 83
Heath, Edward 107
Heroines 45
historicization
  see Brecht, Bertolt
homosexuality 13, 87, 106
House of Un-American Activities
    (HUAC) 22
Huber, Wolfgang 72
Hughes, Ted 91
Hunt, Linda 117–18n. 35

improvisation 40, 85, 91, 93–7
individualism 4, 21, 52, 66–7
Innes, Christopher 68–9
  Modern British Drama 3–4
Irish conflict 106–7, 109

Joint Stock 9–10, 40–1, 91, 94,
    98, 107
Joseph Papp's Public Theatre 75, 83
  see also Top Girls premiere New
    York production

Kennedy, John F. 105
Kennedy, Robert 106

Keyssar, Helene 66, 69
  Feminist Theatre 4
King, Martin Luther (Jr.) 106
Knox, John 9
Komporaly, Jozefina 69
  Staging Motherhood 67
Konopka, Diana 117n. 22
Kritzer, Amelia Howe 62

Labour party 44, 105, 107–8
Lane, Harry 69–70, 96, 102
Lavery, Byrony
  Floorshow 113n.18
Lawson, Nigel 110
Libya, US bombing of 103
Littlewood, Joan
  Oh, What a Lovely War! 105
Logan, Brian 74, 79
'lost children' 46–8, 53–5
  see also motherhood
Lucretius
  The Nature of Things 39
Lyotard, Jean-Francois
  The Postmodern Condition 116n.28

McCarthy, Joseph 22
Madonna, 77, 109
Mahaffey, Valerie 117–18n. 35
Major, John 111
Mamet, David 68
Manville, Lesley 72, 83
Marx, Karl 16, 44
  The Communist Manifesto 18
  see also socialism
media images 85–6
Merrill, Lisa 63
Millett, Kate
  Sexual Politics 107
Miners' Strike (1984) 18–19, 73,
  109

  see also trade unions
monetarism 20
Monstrous Regiment 8–9, 14, 20,
  92, 107, 114n. 23
motherhood 1, 5, 8, 11, 21, 37,
  46–56, 58, 60, 65–67, 86
  abortion 14, 29, 55, 106–7
  miscarriage 6–7, 33, 65
  pregnancy 11, 24, 28, 32, 35,
    46–8, 52–5, 96, 106
multiple-role casting 2, 9–10,
  40–1, 68–9, 77–8, 82, 89–90,
  101

National Organization for Women
  (NOW) 17, 105
National Theatre, London 11,
  105, 116n. 1
Nightingale, Benedict 3, 74
Nijo, Lady (as historical figure)
  23–5, 30–1, 38
non-linear play structure 2, 41–2,
  44, 60, 68, 88
nuclear war 26, 33, 70, 102

O'Connor, Isabell Monk 77–8
Out of Joint Theatre Company 10
overlapping dialogue 2, 10, 60–1,
  71–2, 75, 91
Oxford University 5–6, 13–14, 20

Pankratz, Annette 65
patriarchy 10, 16, 48, 61, 64, 72
'personal is political' 7, 13, 64
Petrarch, Francesco 39
  'Tale of Griselda' 115n. 14
Pinter, Harold 8
Pope Clement VIII 38
Pope Joan controversy 23–4, 30,
  38–9

postmodernism 44–5
Prichard, Rebecca
  Essex Girls 116n. 38
privatization 20

race 10, 16, 64, 77–8, 90–1, 101,
  109
Ravenhill, Mark 4, 67–8
  Shopping and Fucking 4
Reagan, Ronald 21–2, 89, 109
realism 75, 82
Reinelt, Janelle 43, 63
  After Brecht: British Epic Theatre
  43
Republican party 81, 87, 109
Rich, Frank 75–6
Roe versus Wade 17, 107
Rolling Stones, The 105
Rosefeldt, Paul 61
Rossenstein, Brad 75, 78
Rowbotham, Sheila 19
Royal Court Theatre 3–4, 7–8, 10,
  72, 75, 83–4, 88, 106, 109,
  111
Royal Shakespeare Company 11
Rubik, Margarete 61–2, 69
Rumens, Carol 72

Schneider, Melody 61–3
Second Stride 12
sexism 8, 9, 17, 67
  see also 'glass ceiling', patriarchy
Sharp, Lesley 92
Sharrock, Thea 73, 84
socialism 1, 5, 13, 15–20, 37, 44,
  60, 62–4, 81, 87–8
  proletariat 18
  see also Marx, Karl
Spencer, Lady Diana 109
Spice Girls, The 68

Stafford-Clark, Max 3, 9–11, 40,
  42, 71–2, 75, 79, 82–3, 85,
  91–2, 96, 98, 108, 111
  see also Top Girls premiere
  London (Royal Court Theatre)
Stangl, Casy 77–8
  see also Top Girls revival Guthrie
  Theater
'state of the nation' plays 37, 73,
  75
Streisand, Barbara 77

Taylor, Gwen 83
Taylor, John Russell 75
Taylor, Paul 91
taxation 20–2, 110–11
terrorism 8, 103
Thatcher, Margaret / Thatcherism
  1–2, 16, 19– 22, 28, 33, 44,
  46, 56, 64–8, 70–4, 76, 81,
  86–8, 98, 102–3, 107–9
  biographical background 14,
  19–20
  election 1, 13, 19, 108
  and the Miner's strike (1984)
  18–19, 73, 109
  resignation 68, 79, 111
  'Thatcher's Children' 66, 114n.
  41
Top Girls productions
  film version (BBC, Open University) 71, 79–82, 90, 98, 111
  premieres
  Austrian (Ensemble Theatre,
  Vienna) 72, 83, 103, 117n.
  7
  German (Schauspielhaus,
  Cologne) 78, 83
  Greek (National Theatre,
  Athens) 78, 83

London, (Royal Court Theatre)   17, 21–2, 40, 60, 67, 71–2, 83, 109
New York (Public Theater)   3, 75–6, 83
revivals   71–9, 82–5, 111
Battersea Arts Centre (BAC), London   73, 84
Guthrie Theater, Minneapolis   77–8, 81, 90
Williamstown Theatre Festival, Massachusetts   76
trade unions   17, 19, 21–2, 44, 56
see also Miners' Strike (1984), air traffic controllers' strike

unemployment   21, 107, 109
United States, relationship with the UK   12–13, 21–2, 70, 89, 102–3
USSR   22, 88, 109–10
see also Cold War

Vietnam War   14, 105–7

Wade, Laura   114n.21
Wakefield, Lou   83
Walter, Natasha
New Feminism, The   68
Wandor, Michelene   64
Floorshow   113n. 18
Watergate scandal   107
Weir, Alison   77
welfare state   20

Wertenbaker, Timberlake
Our Country's Good   8, 64, 110
Whelehan, Imelda   67–8
Overloaded: Popular Culture and the Future of Feminism   67
Wilson, Harold   105, 107
Windsor, Prince Charles   109
'Winter of Discontent'   108
women's liberation movement   13–14, 16–17
Miss America Contest   14
Miss World Contest   14, 107
Ruskin College women's conference   13–14
'sisterhood'   15–16, 21, 54
Women's Press   107
Women's Theatre Group   107
My Mother Says I Never Should   14
Women's Festival, Almost Free Theatre   107
see also feminism
Woodstock   106
working class community   16, 26, 28–33, 39, 43–4, 51–2, 55–7, 59, 62–3, 68, 78, 81, 95
see also class conflict
working woman
see career woman

1980s, The   1–4, 8, 13, 17–18, 21–3, 33, 44, 57, 66, 72–3, 76, 80, 85–8, 96, 109–10